Starving Ethiopians trek to Bati camp, hoping to find aid.

Fleeing Vietnamese are rescued in the South China Sea by a Médecins du Monde rescue boat.

An Angolan civilian struggles to cross the Cunene River to safety in South West Africa, after the fall of Angola in 1975.

A Ugandan boy, displaced by civil war, is lifted onto the back of a U.N. truck commandeered to relocate him and his countrymen to a resettlement village in northern Uganda.

Iranian students, caught in the aftermath of their country's revolution, fight deportation from Greece.

FORCE

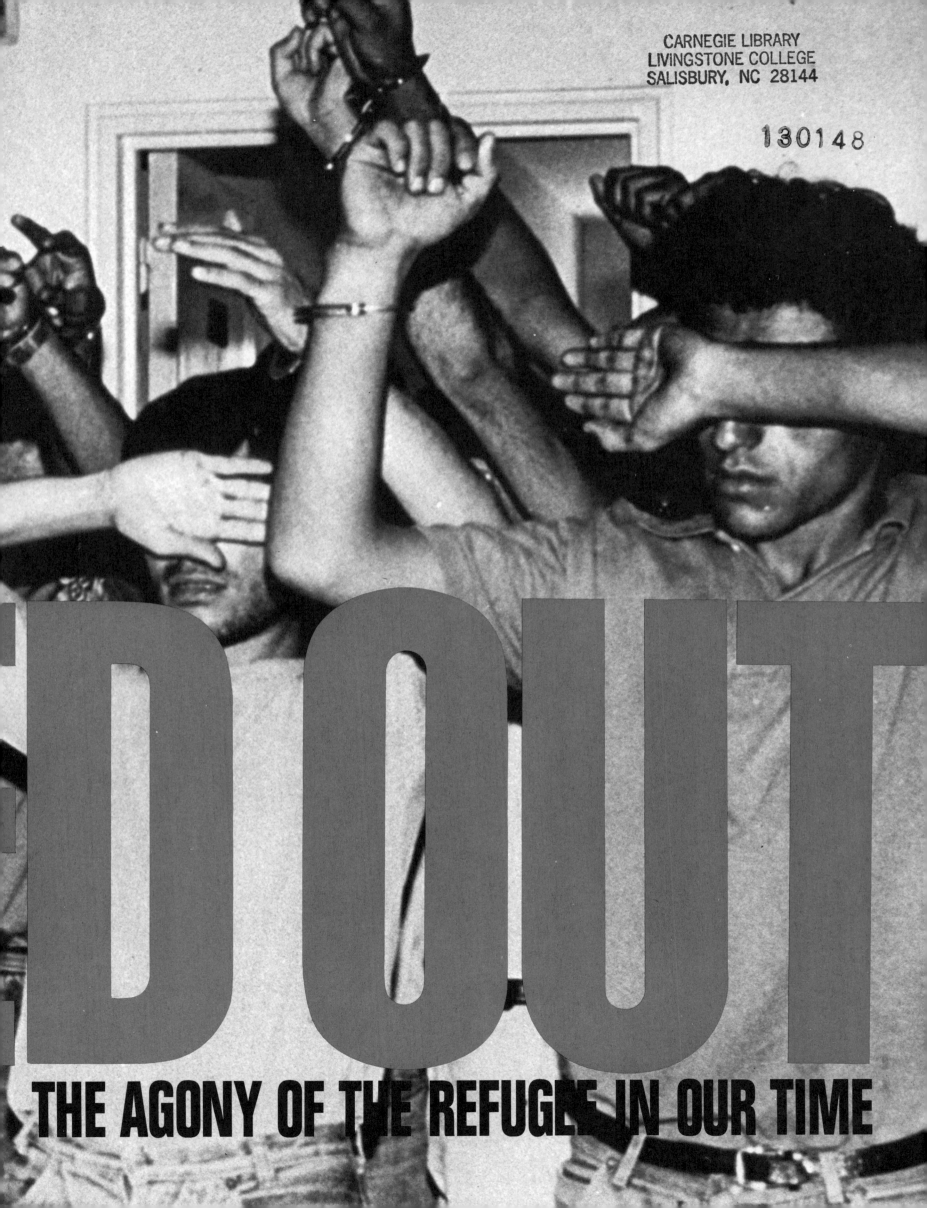

DOUT

THE AGONY OF THE REFUGEE IN OUR TIME

An East Berlin soldier leaps over a barbed-wire barricade to seek asylum in West Berlin.

BY
CAROLE KISMARIC

PUBLISHED BY
HUMAN RIGHTS WATCH
AND
THE J. M. KAPLAN FUND

IN ASSOCIATION WITH
WILLIAM MORROW & CO.
W. W. NORTON & CO.
PENGUIN BOOKS LTD.
RANDOM HOUSE, INC.

H—7)HILLSBORO INLET,Fla.Oct.26—REFUGEE BOAT TRAGEDY—Deerfield Beach police officer Joe Dente and lifeguard Butch Santonastaso look at some of the Haitians who drowned Monday off Hillsboro Inlet north of Fort Lauderdale when their overloaded boat swamped near shore. More than sixty Haitians were aboard the vessel. Thirty-three Haitians survived the ordeal by swimming ashore.(AP LASERPHOTO)(kaw21700mbr/News—Bill Reinke)1981 MIAMI HERALD, BOCA NEWS, HOMESTEAD NEWS LEADER OUT, TV OUT,MO, MO

Fleeing repression and poverty in their homeland, drowned Haitians lie on a Florida beach after their overloaded boat swamped near shore.

Tamils at Heathrow Airport, England, demonstrate against their return to war-torn Sri Lanka.

The work of the Human Rights Watch Committees is greatly respected by our foundation; it has inspired this book. Fact gatherers, public educators, and advocates, the Watches have, in a few short years, become a force in the universal cause of human rights.

Among their concerns is the worsening condition of the refugee. With the Committees we wondered—because statistics can blur into meaninglessness—how the refugee's anguish might be brought home. The right publication could help, we thought.

Here it is, we believe—the achievement of many hands, many voices. Carole Kismaric is the person who, over two hard-working years, largely shaped the book.

Forced Out owes its character also to Aryeh Neier, vice-chairman of the Watch Committees. From his colleagues, Jeri Laber and Arthur Helton, came testimony and a helpful critical eye. Susan Jonas, editorial associate, made significant contributions to its every aspect.

Roland Algrant brought *Forced Out* from the shade of the non-profit world into the light of international publishing by proposing that four distinguished publishers join in consortium for the book, as a matter of conscience. We thank Lawrence Hughes of William Morrow; James Mairs of W. W. Norton; Peter Mayer and Peter Carson of Penguin Books, Ltd.; and Robert Bernstein and Peter Osnos of Random House.

To all these, our co-workers and friends, as well as to the many other people who have become involved with *Forced Out*—and to the readers—the Trustees of our Fund wish to express their admiration and appreciation.

JOAN K. DAVIDSON, President, The J. M. Kaplan Fund

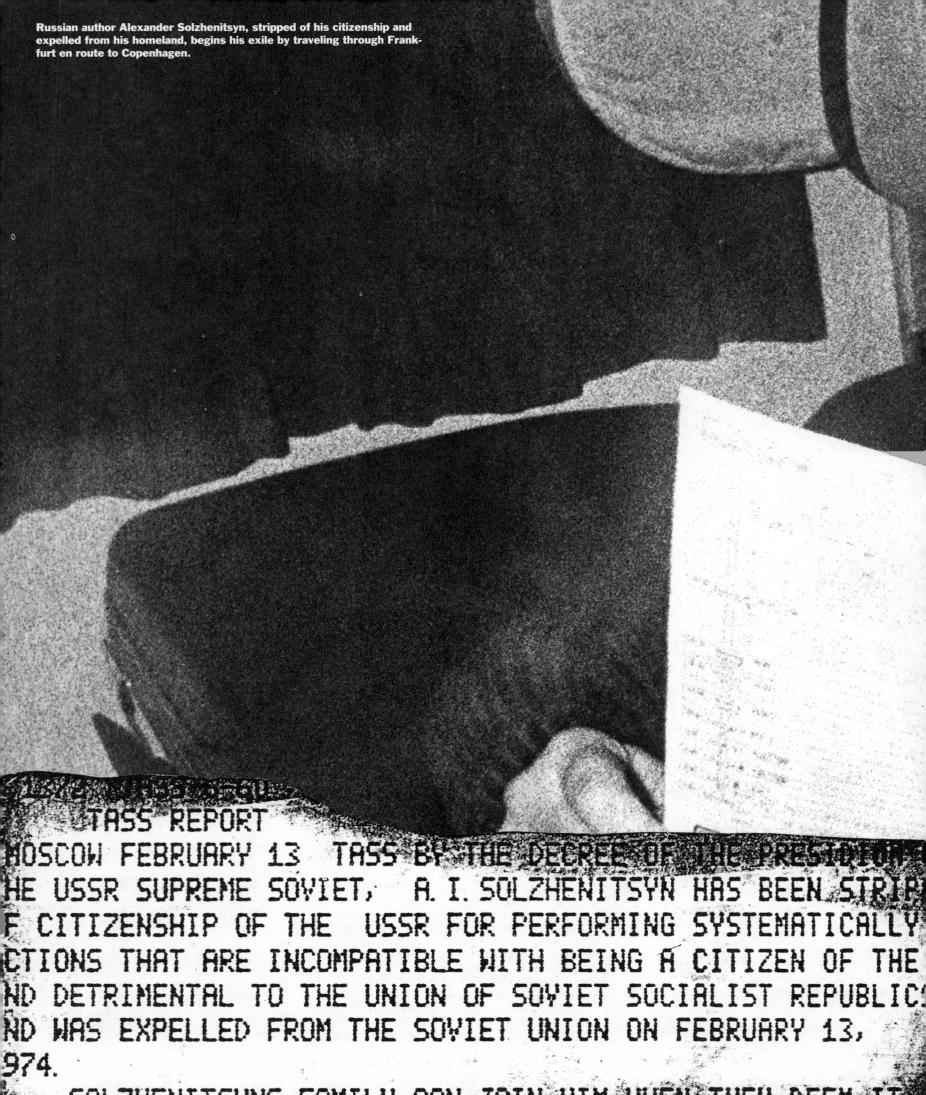

Russian author Alexander Solzhenitsyn, stripped of his citizenship and expelled from his homeland, begins his exile by traveling through Frankfurt en route to Copenhagen.

TASS REPORT
MOSCOW FEBRUARY 13   TASS BY THE DECREE OF THE PRESIDIUM
HE USSR SUPREME SOVIET,   A. I. SOLZHENITSYN HAS BEEN STRIP
F CITIZENSHIP OF THE   USSR FOR PERFORMING SYSTEMATICALLY
CTIONS THAT ARE INCOMPATIBLE WITH BEING A CITIZEN OF THE
ND DETRIMENTAL TO THE UNION OF SOVIET SOCIALIST REPUBLIC
ND WAS EXPELLED FROM THE SOVIET UNION ON FEBRUARY 13,
974.

    SOLZHENITSYNS FAMILY CAN JOIN HIM WHEN THEY DEEM IT
ECESSARY.   ITEM ENDS

WITH EYEWITNESS
ACCOUNTS BY REFUGEES
FROM AFGHANISTAN
CAMBODIA
EL SALVADOR ETHIOPIA
GUATEMALA HAITI
IRAN IRAQ LAOS
MOZAMBIQUE NAMIBIA
NICARAGUA PALESTINE
SOUTH AFRICA
UGANDA URUGUAY
SOVIET UNION
AND VIETNAM

COMMENTARY BY
WILLIAM SHAWCROSS

AND TEXTS BY
MARK MALLOCH BROWN
BILL FRELICK
ARTHUR HELTON
JERI LABER
AND ARYEH NEIER

A Tigrayan mother and child, terrorized by strafing Ethiopian MIG's, flee by night into Sudan.

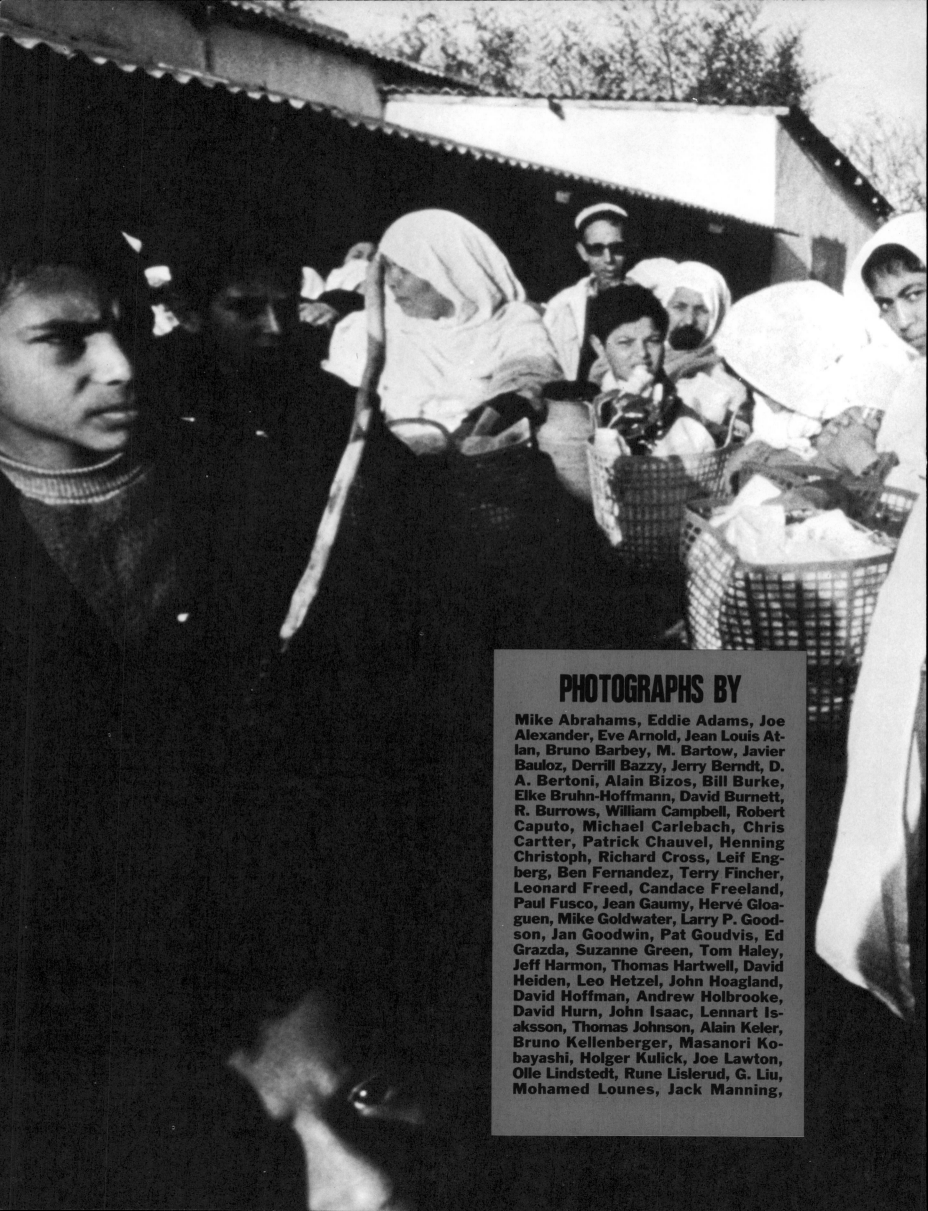

PHOTOGRAPHS BY

Mike Abrahams, Eddie Adams, Joe Alexander, Eve Arnold, Jean Louis Atlan, Bruno Barbey, M. Bartow, Javier Bauloz, Derrill Bazzy, Jerry Berndt, D. A. Bertoni, Alain Bizos, Bill Burke, Elke Bruhn-Hoffmann, David Burnett, R. Burrows, William Campbell, Robert Caputo, Michael Carlebach, Chris Cartter, Patrick Chauvel, Henning Christoph, Richard Cross, Leif Engberg, Ben Fernandez, Terry Fincher, Leonard Freed, Candace Freeland, Paul Fusco, Jean Gaumy, Hervé Gloaguen, Mike Goldwater, Larry P. Goodson, Jan Goodwin, Pat Goudvis, Ed Grazda, Suzanne Green, Tom Haley, Jeff Harmon, Thomas Hartwell, David Heiden, Leo Hetzel, John Hoagland, David Hoffman, Andrew Holbrooke, David Hurn, John Isaac, Lennart Isaksson, Thomas Johnson, Alain Keler, Bruno Kellenberger, Masanori Kobayashi, Holger Kulick, Joe Lawton, Olle Lindstedt, Rune Lislerud, G. Liu, Mohamed Lounes, Jack Manning,

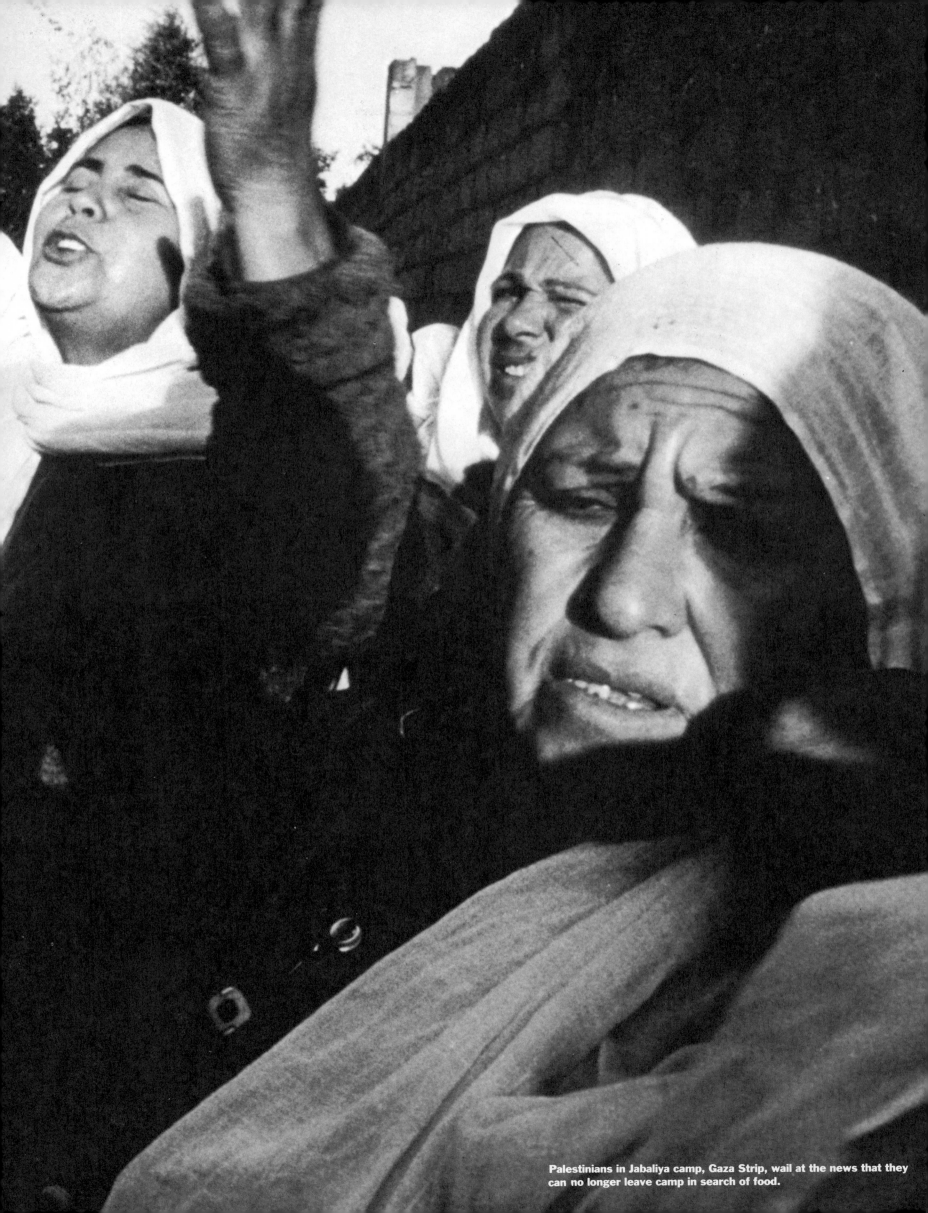

Palestinians in Jabaliya camp, Gaza Strip, wail at the news that they can no longer leave camp in search of food.

Salvadoran refugees in Albuquerque, New Mexico, contact religious workers offering them protection in defiance of United States law.

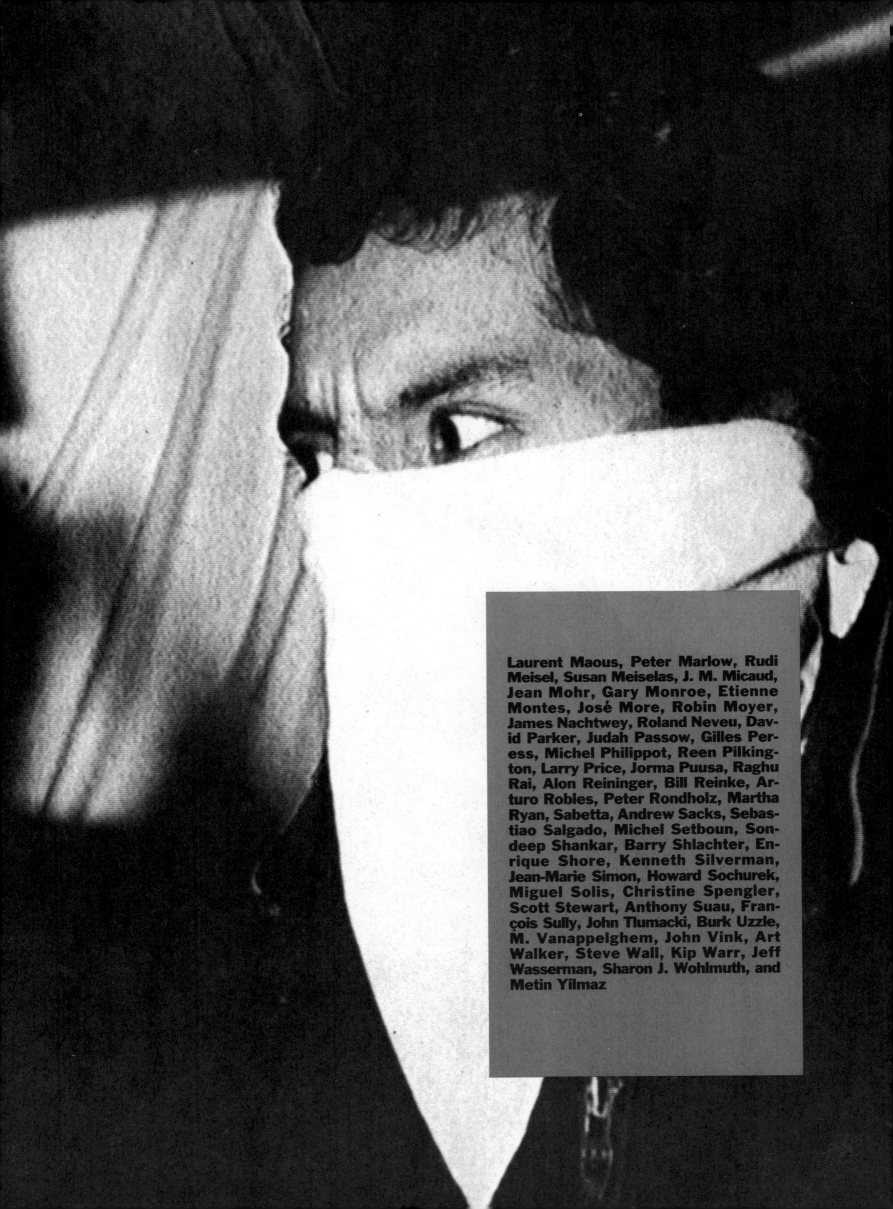

Laurent Maous, Peter Marlow, Rudi Meisel, Susan Meiselas, J. M. Micaud, Jean Mohr, Gary Monroe, Etienne Montes, José More, Robin Moyer, James Nachtwey, Roland Neveu, David Parker, Judah Passow, Gilles Peress, Michel Philippot, Reen Pilkington, Larry Price, Jorma Puusa, Raghu Rai, Alon Reininger, Bill Reinke, Arturo Robles, Peter Rondholz, Martha Ryan, Sabetta, Andrew Sacks, Sebastiao Salgado, Michel Setboun, Sondeep Shankar, Barry Shlachter, Enrique Shore, Kenneth Silverman, Jean-Marie Simon, Howard Sochurek, Miguel Solis, Christine Spengler, Scott Stewart, Anthony Suau, François Sully, John Tlumacki, Burk Uzzle, M. Vanappelghem, John Vink, Art Walker, Steve Wall, Kip Warr, Jeff Wasserman, Sharon J. Wohlmuth, and Metin Yilmaz

Displaced Afghans trudge through heavy snow as they cross the border into Pakistan two months after the Soviet invasion in 1979.

Cambodian children in a refugee camp along the Thai-Cambodian border
chase a truck delivering food.
Overleaf: Site 2 camp, Thailand.

Some 60,000 female refugees at Site 2 camp in Thailand sit for hours in the sun, as they are counted by officials who will give them food rations.

FROM THE ARCHIVES OF

Agence VU, Agence France Presse, Alpha, American Committee for Human Rights, Amnesty International, Archive Pictures, Athens Press, Black Star, "The Boston Globe," Camera Press, "The Chicago Tribune," Contact Press Images, Committee for a Free Afghanistan, Gamma-Liaison, "The Globe and Mail" (Toronto), Grassroots International, JB Pictures, Magnum Photos, "The Miami News," Mira Agency, Network, "The New York Times," "News/Sun Sentinel" (Fort Lauderdale), Oxfam America, Photoreporters, Pressens Bild, Photographers International, Rapho, Reuters, Ringier Dokumentationszentrum, Samfoto, Sipa Press, Sygma, Time-Life Picture Collection, United Nations, United Nations High Commissioner for Refugees, United Nations Relief and Works Agency, UPI/Bettmann, Visum, Visions Photo Group, Wheeler Pictures, Wide World, and Woodfin Camp & Associates.

An anti-riot policeman strikes a Cuban refugee making his way to the United Nations High Commissioner for Refugees Mission in Lima, Peru.

CONTENTS

A TOURIST IN THE REFUGEE WORLD

WILLIAM SHAWCROSS

There is a wealth of good trips to be had from refugees. I am not referring to the mundane fact that refugees have by definition themselves made trips. I mean that the refugee world offers a lot of tourist potential. I am surprised that it has not been more assiduously exploited. Many of the locations are, after all, fabulous. Miami beaches—"Relax in Five-Star Luxury with a Martini on the Sand"—for the Haitians. Hong Kong markets—"Fabulous Shopping"—for the Vietnamese. Palm trees in Sri Lanka or southern India—"The Temple Bells Are Calling"—for the Tamils. Vienna—"City of Strauss, Freud, and Waldheim"—for Poles and other East Europeans. Honduras—"Exotic Peoples, Pina Coladas, and Wonderful Warmth"—for Nicaraguans, Salvadorans, and others.

When you think of it, there is no end of possible journeys to see these strange people who have either risked everything to seek a more secure future or have been driven from their homes by war, persecution, famine, or flood. Fourteen million refugees scattered over 100 countries. What a marvelous theme for a tour! The airlines should offer a "Round the World Special" to fit in as many as possible. "From the First World to the Fourth World. Buy Now at Bargain Prices. Return Flights All Bookable!" Especially important, this last guarantee, for anyone visiting refugees. It's no joke to be caught in a camp without an onward booking.

I, myself, am a tourist of refugee worlds. For ten years after 1975 I made many trips to Thailand. I was trying to learn and then to write about what was going on in Cambodia, which lies along Thailand's eastern border. In the event, I wrote two books about Cambodia.

In Bangkok I stayed in comfortable hotels and ate delicious food. From the city I would take a car or sometimes a bus and drive east a few hundred kilometers to the Cambodian border to visit the camps of refugees who had fled from Cambodia and Vietnam.

By 1975 there were only a few thousand Cambodians there, the first to escape the bloody rule of the Khmer Rouge, who had won victory in April 1975. Sitting in bamboo huts and guarded by Thai soldiers, they told terrifying tales of Khmer Rouge brutality. They described how the communists had emptied all towns at gunpoint, forcing people to start a new life in the countryside; they spoke of death being meted out to anyone suspected of connections with the ancien régime, all traces of which the Khmer Rouge sought to eradicate. People wearing glasses might be clubbed to death to punish them for being "intellectuals."

By the end of 1979 the camps along the border had greatly expanded. Now they held hundreds of thousands of people who had fled Cambodia in the turmoil that followed the Vietnamese overthrow of the Khmer Rouge. The largest Cambodian town in the world at the time was a refugee camp, Khao I Dang, just a few kilometers inside Thailand.

Over the years I talked to scores of refugees about what was going on in their country. I recorded their hopes and fears in my notebook or on my tapes, showed them sympathy—undoubtedly not enough—promised to post letters for them, and returned to Bangkok.

In my hotel room I would start to write up what I had learned. I would call people from the aid agencies—the International Red Cross, Unicef, the United Nations High Commissioner for Refugees—and perhaps, from the embassies most involved—in this case as in so many the U.S. Embassy. Officials told me the numbers, in and out of the camps. They talked about the war in Cambodia, about rates of refugee resettlement—how well country X was doing, how poorly country Y. Some talked about the "pull factor"—the theory that the very existence of resettlement programs in the West encouraged people to leave who would otherwise have stayed home. In other words, Vietnamese were being tempted out onto the South China Sea by promises of homes in California.

In other offices, strewn with paper, Thai officials, many of them military men, told me of the sacrifices Thailand was incurring on behalf of the refugees it tolerated on its soil. This was not strictly so. The care and succor of the refugees was all being underwritten by other governments' payments to the international agencies, and Thailand actually benefited from the policy that Thai officials called "the open door" but that in fact was only ajar. Apart from the money and international political support the refugees brought Thailand, their presence along the border created a human buffer between the Thai and Vietnamese armies with which the Thai military felt very comfortable.

My bag filled with whatever documents had been pressed upon me or that I had solicited, I returned to my hotel. I wrote some more. With friends I ate more delicious meals. Sometimes I literally cleaned the dust or the mud of the camps off my shoes, and with it some of the squalor, and I flew west towards home. There, in the comfort and security and familiarity with which I was surrounded, I wrote some more and hoped that in so doing I contributed a little to the understanding of the problem. But I knew it was only a mite.

Again, as a refugee tourist in the Middle East, I have driven from Damascus in a group taxi through dozens of ancient, stone-built villages in the Shouf Mountains that had for centuries been homes but in the last decade have been blasted away by shells. These settlements were deserted now; only the wreckage remained.

Across the border called the Green Line, which savagely divides the eastern and western halves of Beirut, I have seen a little of the malice, destruction, and indifference in which thousands upon thousands of people live in Sabra, Chattila, and Bourj al Barajneh. In a sense all Beirutis are refugees. On the beach in West Beirut, people still lay in the sun below the carcasses of burnt-out hotels, destroyed in the internecine fighting. In the shops people still conducted the commerce of every day life. But the beaches were frequently shelled at random by one or the other faction in the hills behind the town, and shops were often exploded by wantonly placed car bombs. In recent years great publicity has been given to the two dozen or more western hostages cruelly interred in the labyrinthine refugee camp slums of West Beirut. At the same time, thousands upon thousands of Lebanese have been captured by various warlords. And millions have had their lives destroyed.

In Ethiopia I have seen the steady anguish with which armies of starving people have walked for hundreds of miles across the wastelands of the northern provinces to attend feeding centers run by the government or western agencies. I have also seen in the south a few of the villages in which many thousands of northerners have been "resettled" by the government. Since many of the people moved south had been removed by force from their homes, it was often argued that "deported" was a more apt word than "resettled" for what had happened to them. Many had come from the provinces of Tigray where there was not only drought but an insurrection against the Addis Ababa regime; "resettlement" was an obvious way of denying manpower to the rebels.

Once I flew from Addis in a Royal Air Force transport plane that was participating in an airdrop of grain to starving villagers in another northern Ethiopian province. These people, too, had walked for scores of miles up and down fantastic soaring crags and valleys to retrieve sacks dropped from the low-flying aircraft. As they fell, many sacks burst open and the people swept the grass with twigs to make sure that no precious grains were wasted. It was a long day.

Those of us—journalists, western aid workers, R.A.F. men—who had flown in from Addis had been told to bring our own lunch boxes. My hotel had provided roast chicken and sweet cakes. The R.A.F. men ate chocolate bars and drank tea from a thermos; the thin Africans laboriously gathered the individual grains.

I have driven through the Sahara into southern Algeria with a television crew, in cars filled with cans and boxes of English food to add the taste of home cooking to the desert campfire. There in the sand I have seen rows upon rows of tents in which are housed some of those people who have fled from the drought of countries like Mali further south. Across the Algerian border in Niger, I have talked to nomads who have been forced by drought, or government policy, to abandon their transient way of life, to sell or to kill their livestock and to squat around the towns, beggars not choosers.

In all of these places I have been, and I have felt like a voyeur. I do not find the experience comfortable or reassuring. In fact it is distasteful. It sometimes seems a form of slumming which is supposed to be made respectable by the fact that my colleagues and I carry cameras or typewriters.

From all of these places, which together are more typical of the world today than where I live in London, I have been able to do the one thing which almost none of those whom I have met can do: Go home, blessed home. One of the first poems British schoolchildren are taught is Robert Browning's:

"I remember, I remember, the house where I was born, The little window where the sun came peeping through at morn."

In this book the poignant voices of refugees recall their lost homes, their precious rituals forcibly abandoned, and demonstrate that all is memory. Memory is, in the end, all they have left. And their dependence upon attitudes and policies in the world to their west or their north is terrifying.

For example, back in 1979 the boat people captured western (northern) imagination. So did the Ethiopians in 1984. Spontaneous albeit brief outpouring of western compassion and aid can help relieve immediate suffering. But such outbursts do not often alleviate the long-term causes of despair and conflict. Indeed they sometimes reinforce them. This happened along the Thai-Cambodian border, where armies of both sides in the civil war in Cambodia were sustained by western food aid. There are still 300,000 people living in a vicious limbo land along the border today. The Khmer Rouge, a broken force after the Vietnamese invasion of 1978—79, have been rebuilt into the most powerful guerrilla army in the country. Now, in 1988, with the Vietnamese apparently at least ready to withdraw, there will be real difficulties in preventing the Khmer Rouge from regaining power. Similarly, in Ethiopia both the government in Addis Ababa and the rebel secessionists in Eritrea and Tigray were reinforced by the massive donations of aid in 1984—85. In 1988 Ethiopia had been further reduced by war, as well as drought, and faced more years of ferocious famine. But the satellites had moved on. They always do.

When I was trying to write these words, the British newspapers carried several different stories about boat people. The first, from a camp in Thailand, reported that the Thai government had again been pushing Vietnamese back out to sea. Those who did make it past naval patrols and brutal pirates to Thai beaches were not now to be allowed to continue their journeys to a permanent new home. They would be locked forever on the beach. These people had taken the immense and horrifying decision to leave their homes. They had bribed or braved their way out of their country, risked death on the sea in frail craft, reached what they hoped would be some sort of safe transit point on their journey—only to be told that it was the end of the road. The place they had left behind, for all its faults, was never a prison like this. At the time of the Thai announcement, there were 3,000 boat people on the beaches and thousands more were expected to arrive.

At the same time, the Hong Kong government, under British direction, announced that it would tow back to sea those Vietnamese whom it did not consider "real," political refugees, and would repatriate others.

In the summer of 1979 when the plight of the boat people was at its height, with scores of thousands fleeing every day from Vietnam, their cause was embraced and at the same time their predicament was extensively exploited by western governments to demonstrate the cruelty of Vietnamese communism.

But the flow of refugees did not conveniently end once they had demonstrated the nature of Hanoi's rule. Indeed, the boat people have continued to flee a country where economic deprivation and starvation have joined political repression as reasons for flight. Since 1981 219,000 Vietnamese have landed on foreign shores. Their plight is no longer of much interest in the West. Now they are labeled mere "economic migrants."

In the summer of 1988 a group of boat people arrived in the Philippines and at once horrific charges of murder and cannibalism were leveled by the survivors. One report mentioned that the cannibalism had occurred after the boat people had used all the water and food that had been given them by a U.S. navy vessel. Back in 1979 U.S navy ships had been dispatched to the South China Sea precisely to search for and rescue boat people. A few years later they were merely given a few snacks and pushed back to the ocean alone.

By the fall of 1988 it had become clear that the Hong Kong government, in concert with others of Southeast Asia, was embarking upon a plan for the forcible repatriation of boat people. One journalist compared this plan to the forced repatriation of the Cossacks to the Soviet Union and death after World War II. But was there an outcry? Not a murmur.

One reason for this fall in interest is a curious new malady that is said to be afflicting more and more people and institutions throughout the world. It is called Compassion Fatigue. It is very often fatal.

Like AIDS, Compassion Fatigue is a contemporary sickness. The symptoms are first a rush of concern for a distant and obviously suffering group, followed by tedium and a feeling of withdrawal that sometimes descends into disdain. Those who suffer from Compassion Fatigue are compelled first to express and then to deny sympathy. Thus, today's cause becomes tomorrow's bore. There are fashions for refugees and for disasters. They change fast. Images that this week command attention and approval are next week cast impatiently aside.

Compassion Fatigue is nurtured by the speed and plethora of communications that bewilder and disorient people everywhere. "Dallas" and "Dynasty," images of first world excess and avarice, are beamed down from satellites to the poor of the third and fourth worlds. At the same time images of war and the suffering of refugees are beamed up from those worlds and back into the living rooms of the relatively rich, to offer a fleeting diversion between the soaps.

Compassion Fatigue is a truly terrifying sickness. Those it afflicts do not waste away physically—it is their humanity that is harmed. The fatalities are among those with whom the infected deal, or fail to deal: refugees or the starving, whose plights are first taken up and then simply ignored.

Refugees are defined by the 1951 United Nations Convention as individuals fleeing well-founded fear of persecution. Today people also flee in large groups, and they flee violence as well as persecution. And of course, it is true that some of them are "economic migrants;" this is inevitable. As western, particularly American culture becomes global, more and more people from all over the world will inevitably dream of resettling in Orange County, which seems from afar to be simply a suburb of South Fork. To first entice them and then to cast them out is grotesque.

Perhaps, in this context, the 1951 definition needs to be reconsidered. What we need to understand better and to accept is the unprecedented responsibilities that are incumbent upon the richer or more powerful nations in a world which is more inextricably intertwined than ever. First there is the fact that images of the West serve as a lure to people who can see only the most dismal prospects at home. This is particularly true of people like the Vietnamese, or many in Central America, who have in one way or another been caught in the embrace of western civilization or ambition. Forgive me for concentrating on Southeast Asia, but it is the area with which I am most familiar and furthermore, many of its lessons apply equally to other parts of the globe. For us to encourage the boat people as sailors to freedom in 1979 and then to denounce and reject them a few years later as mere "economic migrants" demonstrates a condition far worse than any fatigue. Such an attitude fails to acknowledge in any way that the predicaments of others may be related to our own, or at least to our governments' actions.

Thousands of those who flee today may well be attempting to escape the wretched poverty into which the country has sunk since the end of the war in 1975. One reason for that poverty is that Vietnam has been denied almost all international aid since its invasion of Cambodia at the end of 1978. The Vietnamese government may well bear the primary responsibility for the impasse that followed, but it is one that Vietnam's enemies, especially China and Thailand, have also nurtured, with western support. The bleeding of Vietnam has been an aim of policy, and today's boat people are, at least in part, a consequence of that policy. Thus it is that there are prisons for refugees in Hong Kong. Thus it is that Thai beaches are divided into those that incarcerate Vietnamese who venture bravely across the South China Sea in frail craft and those that are playgrounds for tourists who tumble frivolously out of their jumbo jets.

From the specifics of Vietnam and Cambodia comes a general point. The uprooting of people and the creation of refugees is very often not just a byproduct of war or starvation but a deliberate act of government policy. Refugees are a commodity to be traded for political ends. There is perhaps nothing new about this—those in power have always sought to corral or to disperse ordinary people. But in the last decades of the twentieth century, while the nuclear rivalry of the superpowers has kept war out of one traditional battleground—Europe—proxy wars or surrogate conflicts have been fought all over other parts of the world in the pursuit of that same rivalry. Sometimes, as in the Horn of Africa, the patrons have changed sides and an "outpost of democracy" has suddenly become a "Soviet satellite." Such relabeling has usually meant nothing to the people involved. The fighting over them has continued, and their lives have been betrayed in the name of a different dogma.

A real picture of the world today would show millions of homeless men, women, and children, being forced from north, south, east, and west—away from their homes, often away from their relatives—marching, stopping, marching; sailing, landing, sailing; shuttling, pausing, shuffling—often with no clear destination in sight, with little hope of return.

This is a phenomenon that must be considered and deplored. It is integral to the world in which we live, a world in which many of us live comfortably and many others are always in restless torment. It is a phenomenon that is intolerable.

WHO ARE THE REFUGEES: WHERE DO THEY GO?

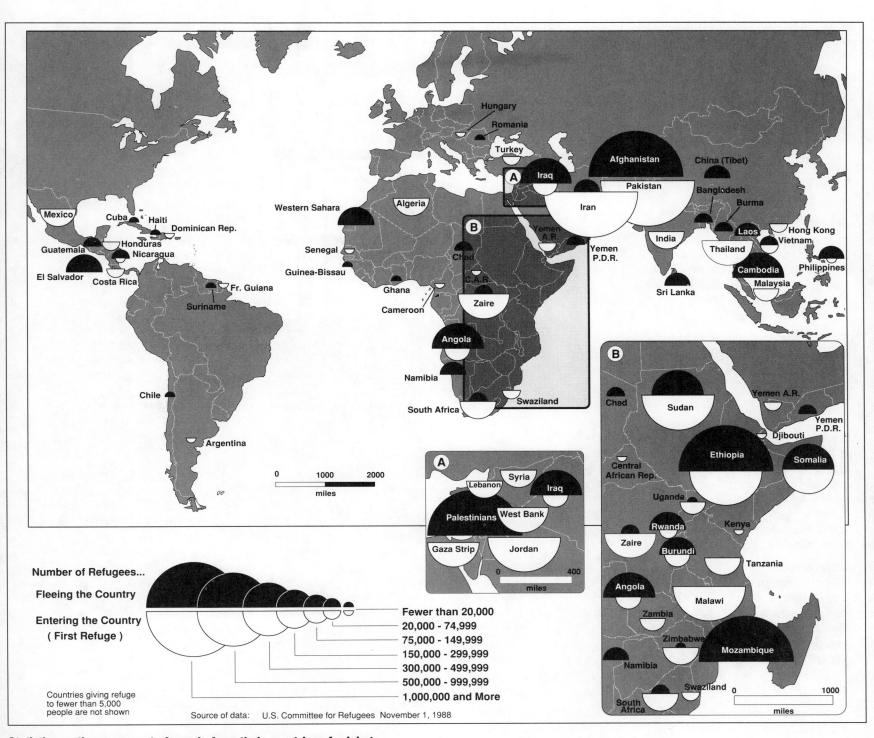

Number of Refugees...

Fleeing the Country

Entering the Country
(First Refuge)

Fewer than 20,000
20,000 - 74,999
75,000 - 149,999
150,000 - 299,999
300,000 - 499,999
500,000 - 999,999
1,000,000 and More

Countries giving refuge
to fewer than 5,000
people are not shown

Source of data: U.S. Committee for Refugees November 1, 1988

**Statistics on the movement of people from their countries of origin to
receiving host countries are listed on page 119.**

1.
FORCED TO FLEE: GOVERNMENTS AGAINST THEIR OWN PEOPLE

Nicaraguan children meet up with Sandinista Army regulars patrolling the countryside. The Sandinista government has fought a guerrilla war against some 15,000 *contras*, supported by the United States.

REMEMBERING HOME

Vietnamese village on the Caman Peninsula, Vietnam.

OUR WAYS WERE VERY OLD

I was born in a small village in the center of Vietnam. It was an isolated village, where almost all the people were farmers, living on what they could grow in their own rice fields. They prepared those rice fields with wooden ploughs, drawn by buffalo. Their fathers had prepared the fields identically for 2,000 years.

The villagers were very good-hearted people, only different from those of other villages in that they were Catholic, instead of Buddhist. As I grew up, I learned that I was the fourth generation of a Catholic family, which had begun with my great-grandmother, who had been persecuted for her faith and had escaped from her native village in the time of the Emperor Tuduc. My great-grandmother's family sailed south, following closely along the coastline, looking for refuge. Finally, her boat with others put into land. She settled down in what I knew as my village, and a small brick church was built for worship. This was the place where I uttered my first cry, and this was where I grew up. This is the village of my memories.

My house stood just in front of the church. It

was a small dwelling with a thatched roof, made of straight trees that were smoothly polished. Cats and mice played hide-and-seek on the roof so continuously that my father had to make a new roof every two years: the old one leaked too badly. Living in that house, I heard the feet on the roof, and beyond them the roar of the wild sea behind the dunes. Whenever the rice crops were planted here and there in the fields, the sweet sounds of a folksong rose up, sung by a girl bending, planting the rice:

> Look upward, so high the sky!
> Look downward, so vast the earth!
> Look beyond, the river so long!
> I wish we could become a nice couple,
> Come hither, let me whisper some words,
> Do not stand near anyone else, when I leave you.

The villagers planted and threshed rice as our ancestors had done forever. Ears of rice cut in the rice fields were carried home by ox cart, or by a man with a yoke on his shoulders, the two bundles of rice bobbing up and down at his side. In the night, farmers leading two buffalo trod round a great curved heap of rice, the animals crushing the grain from the husk. They worked at night to avoid the heat of the tropical sunshine. A boy always watched. When the working buffalo suddenly stopped, raising their tails taut, the boy rushed forward with a scoop, collecting the dung before it fell to soil the grain.

The rice-treading yard was made of dry mud, cracked here and there by the heat. The grain was then ground at the mill made of timber and clay, and drawn by the only other power the villagers had: man. Wind separated the chaff from the grain, and finally, a wooden mortar and pestle were used to pound the rice, taking the bran from the grain to be used for the pigs and chickens.

From my earliest days, the rhythms of all these things made the music of my life. I heard the sounds of the pounding pestles twined with the high-pitched singing of the mothers, as they swung their babies in their hammocks and sang them to sleep. I knew our ways were very old.

SON-HA, South Vietnam

PRACTICALLY A PARADISE

The village is called Chimel; I was born there. Where I live is practically a paradise, the country is so beautiful. There are no big roads and no cars. Only people can reach it. Everything is taken down the mountainside on horseback, or else we carry it ourselves. So, you can see, I live right up in the mountains.

My village has a long history—a long and painful history. The land up there belonged to the government, and you had to get permission to settle there. When you'd get permission, you had to pay a fee so that you could clear the land and then build your house. Through all my parents' efforts in the *fincas,* they managed to get enough money together to pay the fee, and they cleared the land. Of course, it's not easy to make things grow on land that has just been cleared. You don't get a good yield for at least eight or nine years. So my parents cultivated the land, and eight years later it started to produce. We were growing up during this period. I had five older brothers and sisters. I saw my two eldest brothers die from lack of food.

So my parents stayed there. My mother found the trees and our amazing mountains so beautiful. She said that they'd get lost sometimes because the mountains were so high and not a single ray of light fell through the plants. It's very dense. Well, that's where we grew up. We loved our land very, very much, even if we did have to walk for a long time to get to our nearest neighbor.

As very small children, we received an education that is very different from white children, *ladinos.* We worship—or rather not worship,

Campesinos herd sheep in the highlands of San Mateo, Guatemala.

"We love our land very much. Since those people tried to take it away we have grieved very much. My grandfather used to say: 'In the past no one person owned the land. There were no boundaries.'"

but respect—a lot of things to do with the natural world. For instance, to us water is sacred. Our parents tell us when we are very small not to waste water, even when we have it. Water is pure, clean, and gives life to man. Without water we cannot survive, nor could our ancestors have survived. The same goes for the earth. Our parents tell us: "Children, the earth is the mother of man, because she gives him food." This is especially true for us whose life is based on the crops we grow. Our people eat maize, beans, and plants. We can't eat ham, or cheese, or things made with equipment, with machines. We believe that our people are made of maize. We're made of white maize and yellow maize. We must only harm the earth when we are in need. This is why, before we sow our maize, we have to ask the earth's permission. Every part of our culture comes from the earth.

After many years of hard work, when our small bit of land began yielding harvests and our people had a large area under cultivation, the big landowners appeared. They told us we should resign ourselves to working as peons because the land belonged to them. We could stay in our houses, but the land belonged to them. It was not ours. If we didn't agree, they would throw us off.

We didn't have the notion of enemy in our culture until those people arrived to exploit us, oppress us, and discriminate against us. In our community we are all equal. We all have to help one another and share the little we have among us. But we realized in Guatemala there was something inferior and that *we* were the inferior—a sort of animal. Why do they reject us? Why is the Indian not accepted? Why was it the land used to belong to us? Why used our ancestors to live here? Why don't outsiders accept Indian ways?

We began to understand that the rich exploited the poor, our sweat, our labor. We began thinking, with the help of other friends, that our enemies were not only the landowners who lived near us, and above all not just the land-owners who forced us to work and paid us little. It was not only now we are being killed: they had been killing us since we were children, through malnutrition, hunger, poverty. The fact that we were always waiting in offices, always bowing to the authorities, was part of the discrimination we Indians suffered. So was the cultural oppression which tries to divide us by taking away our traditions and prevents unity among our people.

We love our land very much. Since those people tried to take our land away, we have grieved very much. My grandfather used to cry bitterly and say: "In the past no one person owned the land. The land belonged to everyone. There were no boundaries."

RIGOBERTA MENCHU,
Indian leader, Guatemala

TO DIE FOR FAITH AND COUNTRY

The war that we Afghans are waging against the Soviet Union is *jihad,* a holy war, because it is a war to defend the faith and to defend against an infidel, an atheistic power that believes in no religion.

It is the duty of every Afghan to fight back to defend the faith and to defend his country. So that is why it is a great deed to fight *jihad.* God gives to the *mujahedin* who fights *jihad* a special place in paradise. Those who fight *jihad* attain a higher rank than even the prophets. A martyr need not be washed and buried in clean clothes. On the contrary, a martyr can be buried with his clothes soaked in blood. It is an honor not reserved even for prophets and saints.

Another honor, which is given only to martyrs, is that when they die their bodies have no odor. A *mujahedin* martyred in *jihad* will be permitted immediate entry into paradise without having to give an account of his deeds. Almighty God has given the greatest honor to martyrs in that they live forever. Anyone who says that a martyr is really dead is against Islam. All

Afghan *mujahedin* pray in the mountains near Kandahar.

prophets and creatures of God must surrender their souls to the ancient Israel who pulls out souls with a terrible thunderous roar. Not so martyrs. Almighty God removes the soul of a man with no more pain than the bite of a flea. A martyr will give up his soul in such a way as if he was sucking the breast of his mother. God has given these honors only to martyrs. All *mujahedin* know of these honors and they will do nothing but fight *jihad*.

We are fighting *jihad* because we want to go to paradise. We want to be martyred, because paradise awaits those who are martyred. There will be gardens in paradise; there will be many kinds of fruit; there will be wines and pretty boys and pretty girls. Anything you want will be in paradise. All things forbidden the Moslems in this life, a martyr can have in paradise.

We hope to go to paradise, and we hope to convert the infidels so they can also go to paradise. A martyr does not die; he lives forever. We have had many martyrs.

COMMANDER GUL AGHA, Afghanistan

A CULTURE OF ASHES

We arrived home in the evening of the third day of our flight. Everything was changed. Houses that once were beautiful now lay in ruins. The orange and mango trees in the compound were dying, having been severely scorched by the raging fires as they consumed the building. The world was silent. Not a soul was seen, neither was there any sign of animal life. It had rained during the night, and the footmarks left in the wet sand by the heavy boots of the soldiers sent shivers down our spines. The footmarks of death.

At the entrance to our compound, we met the rotting carcass of our once much-loved dog, Bobi, with hundreds of gray flies hovering around the open mouth. There was a bullet hole in the head, and traces of the scattered brain were still visible around the head and in the ear. Nobody talked. We moved on. We put our things down, and I went to what used to be my house.

I stood there gazing at the pile of ashes of destroyed furniture. The ugly sight of the burnt iron bed at one side of the wall did not detain me. I moved to the iron box where I had stored all my precious books. The lock had burnt loose. I tried to open it. The lid came off by itself, and I stared with hot tears in my eyes at the destruction within. My *African Encyclopedia* had been on top of the pile, and the black lump of ashes on top of the ruin must be the pages of the beloved book. It was not the paper itself that provoked tears from my eyes, it was the message, the words, the information in the book—it was the death of the information in the book that made me weep. I thought of the image of Achebe in the book that was now destroyed. I thought about the information under "Solar System." I thought about the information under "Nkrumah," under "Civil War," under "University," and under "Degree." I thought about "Chief Albert Luthuli," about "Jomo Kenyatta," about "Axum," and about "Economics." I thought of as much information in the book as I could remember. I thought about it all.

JAMES APPE, writer, Uganda

A Ugandan returns home to devastation caused by former president Milton Obote's army.

MARTYR OF THE LAND

That day, I woke late. I drank a cup of coffee, listened to the news summary, and went down into the street. It was hot and the streets were somewhat crowded. I made my way to the taxis bound for Jerusalem.

That day, children in a kindergarten bus shouted, "Palestine is Arab" and gave the "V" sign when passing near a border-guard patrol. A woman carrying a basket of thyme and sage searched for a place at the Damascus Gate to display her wares, looking around in fear of the municipal inspectors. A prominent money changer in Nablus informed a number of money changers in towns in the West Bank of the rise in the price of the Jordanian *dinar*. A girl woke, looked around her, and inquired after her brother who slept in the same room. Her mother said sadly: "They took him away."

I got out of the taxi in Al Musrara, stopped in front of a newspaper seller, glanced at the headlines, exchanged a few words, and moved on. There were a number of tourists in the street taking photographs of the women selling vegetables and of shops and landmarks. I reached Salah Eddin Street. One of my colleagues met me. He immediately began: "Have you heard? Someone was killed in Bidia when they tried to confiscate his land." I stopped still.

That day, thousands of young people began a new journey in search of work. A taxi driver told his passengers that the fare had gone up due to the rise in the cost of fuel, and when a young man protested that the government had fixed prices, the driver said: "Go and ride with the government!" A committee decided to form a cooperative to cultivate land on a barren mountain. Two young people gazed at a wall on which they'd written at night, "Down with the Occupation!"—looked around, fearful that their smiles of pride would give them away.

With the colleague who had told me the news I went to a nearby café. We ordered two cups of coffee. My thoughts wandered to Bidia: Confiscation of land . . . did I know the man who had been killed that morning? I may have met him once in the office of a lawyer friend in Nablus. There was a group from one of the villages. The lawyer asked them: "Do you have land registration papers?" One of them answered: "We've been on the land since before

A Palestinian bride and groom at Badawi Camp, Tripoli.

land registration was invented." His words were as sharp as the lines on his face, which was graved with anger and agitation. He looked almost seventy years old, and his eyes flashed enigmatically as he leaned on the stick he carried, holding in his other hand a cigarette, the smoke of which he exhaled in a thin line. Could it be him?

That morning, a new shop opened for selling and renting out videotapes, next door to the new money changer. A young man left prison after doing ten years and threw himself into the arms of his mother, waiting for him at the gates. A boy carried a collection of poetry and anxiously went to a publishing house. An old woman went to a scribe's office to ask him to fill in an application form for a permit for her son and his family to visit the West Bank.

My lawyer friend must have spoken to me about him. The last time we met he told me about the problem of landowners in a village near Nablus, and of his amazement at an old man who came to his office almost daily to ask him what to do about the Israeli companies that wanted to confiscate the land. He may have been the same person who had been killed that day in Bidia. I drank the rest of my coffee and headed for the newspaper office.

That morning, a woman listened to the ten o'clock news on Radio Amman to find out if one of her relatives in exile had died the previous day. A husband told his wife that it was time to have a second child, and she blushed and began to prepare for the night. A farmer went to work on his land and found that settlers had confiscated it. A young man decided he

> "He must have felt that the bulldozers, as he followed their monstrous dismemberment of the soil, were tearing him apart. He must have felt he was losing all justification for existence."

had no future in this country and told the taxi driver on the way to Jerusalem: "Let me off at the American consulate."

In the office I followed up on the news. The man had been killed by bullets of the Israeli border guards as he tried to prevent the Israeli settlers' bulldozers from working on his land. One of our correspondents called and told me the name of the man was Ibrahim Al-Aqra. I asked him to get a picture from the family and some information about him. His age. His children. And details of the matter of his land. When I hung up, I felt depressed. Then I told myself that this profession deadens many feelings and started to think again about Ibrahim Al-Aqra. I wondered what he was feeling at the very moment he set out to prevent the bulldozers from working on his land. He must have felt that the bulldozers, as he followed their monstrous dismemberment of the soil, were tearing *him* apart. An enormous well of memories and small, intimate details must have been destroyed. He must have felt that he was losing all justification for his existence. Perhaps he carried no stone or stick in his hand as he advanced toward the bulldozers and the soldiers, but went to stop them with his body alone.

That morning, a field in a village died of neglect. Patrol soldiers of the Israeli Army stopped a boy in a street in a town and beat him brutally. An artist put the final touches to a painting and began searching for a name for it. A person told a friend that the dowry of the girl he wanted to marry was very high and that it was better to cancel the engagement.

A long time passed before there was any new information about what had happened in Bidia. Israeli radio, in all its languages, gave no clear details. The correspondent for the Nablus area promised to send me a full report in the evening with the picture I wanted. I took my pen and placed a sheet of paper in front of me in order to write an editorial on the killing of Ibrahim Al-Aqra.

On the paper I wrote the title: "Martyr of the Land." Feeling that I was about to write a fervent emotional address, I tore up the paper and threw it in the wastepaper basket. On another sheet I wrote: "Day of Killing in Bidia." I thought, the censor will strike that out. I decided to start writing the article first and then put a title to it. The face of Ibrahim Al-Aqra, as I imagined him, appeared before me. I felt as though the color of the ink in my pen had turned to red and that blood covered the paper. I tried time after time to write one complete sentence. But I failed. My pen betrayed me. I flung it away, apologized to my colleagues, and left the office.

That day, a child uttered his first word and his mother's face beamed. A woman in a village finished embroidering a new dress and showed it proudly to her neighbor. A girl clutched to her chest a school bag containing a flag she spent the whole night sewing to hang in a show in her school. A woman told her husband, smiling, that she believed they would be blessed with a child in a few months. A university student began his fieldwork in research into popular sayings in a village. A prisoner underwent torture and resolved to confess nothing. And Ibrahim Al-Aqra was killed. I failed to write an article. And a child threw a stone at an Israeli military patrol and turned and ran. And disappeared into the alleyways of a refugee camp.

AKRAM HANNIYA, Palestinian writer

Soviet-built M-24 helicopters hover near Somotillo, Nicaragua. Crucial to waging counterinsurgency wars, the Army flies helicopters into remote mountainous regions inhabited by peasants believed to support the guerrillas. War machines, which can fire hundreds of rounds of machine-gun-fire a minute, they also hopscotch infantry around the countryside and perform reconnaissance and rescue missions in normally hostile terrain.

THE TYRANNY OF TERROR: RAVAGING HOMELAND

On April 8 at about nine o'clock in the morning, I saw helicopters landing in the hamlets of Nixtamalapa and Papaturro. When I got home I heard a great noise of machine-gun fire directed against our own hamlet of Guadalupe. With my wife, Petrona, I took our children and started running toward the hill with the rest of the inhabitants.

The next day we stayed hidden, trying to make the children shut up and not make any noise. At about eleven o'clock I suddenly heard a voice shouting, ''Nobody move!'' and at the same time came a tremendous burst of machine-gun fire. We took the children and went running up the hill. We were still being machine-gunned, and they threw fire-bombs at us in order to set fire to the dry bush where the people were trying to hide. I saw my wife grab at a reed stem, with our eighteen-month son in her arms, and then both of them fell dead, hit by machine-gun bullets. At the same time my other three children were hit and fell. I took in my arms my only surviving child, Blanca, aged four, and followed the people in front of me. Running very hard, we managed to cross over the hill and reach a dry ravine.

After resting there for about an hour, we suddenly heard the soldiers approaching and realized we were surrounded. They aimed their guns at us, and the one who seemed to be in command said: ''Nobody move! Lay down your arms!'' We weren't armed, so we answered: ''As the Lord is with us, these are our arms,'' and we embraced the children and pointed to them.

The next day they took us to Santa Cruz Michapa, and on the way the soldiers destroyed the few maize plots that were left, and besides insulting us they were talking to each other so that we would hear, saying they wanted to drink blood and eat meat.

When we got to Santa Cruz Michapa they took us to the courthouse. We were assembled inside the building, and the captain told us: ''I have brought you here together to tell you that nothing is going to happen to you. We are

An army unit patrols the village of Las Voeltas in El Salvador. In the early 1980s, the Salvadoran Army waged a campaign against civilians suspected of supporting the opposition. Some 800 Salvadorans were murdered each month, and by 1987 at least 42,000 had been killed or "disappeared."

going to turn you over to the Red Cross. You must forget the subversives. You can go to San Salvador or back to where you lived before. But each and everyone one of you is going to collaborate with us."

Campesino, El Salvador

The first time they threw us out of our homes was, if I remember rightly, in 1967. First they went into the houses without permission and got all the people out. Then they went in and threw out all our things. I remember that my mother had her silver necklaces, precious keepsakes from my grandmother, but we never saw them again after that. They stole them all. They threw out our cooking utensils, our eathenware cooking pots. They hurled them into the air, and oh, God! They hit the ground and broke into pieces. All our plates, cups, pots. They killed our animals. They killed many of our dogs. To us killing an animal is like killing a person.

RIGOBERTA MENCHU
Indian leader, Guatemala

It was a very sad year. The *Guardia Nacional* and the patrols arrived at midnight, when the people were asleep and weren't expecting them; they surrounded the town and started taking people out of their houses. We're sorry, they would say, but it was the only way to find them all, the boys in their homes. Making fun of us, ridiculing our misfortunes. And what could you do? If you make a move to run for it, they start shooting. No one could run that night, maybe because the boys were still half asleep. "They are only going for a year," the members of the patrol would say to make us feel better, "and they'll be more civilized when we send them back. In the barracks they learn to read and mind their manners," they went on, without looking at anyone, addressing the stones that were us. The year was up but they never came back. No one comes back.

MANLIO ARGUETA, writer, El Salvador

A Nicaraguan woman anxiously tries to decide whether to accept money from *contra* soldiers to whom she has given food. In counterinsurgency war, guerrilla and Army forces vie for the peasants' support. Villagers are often the only source of food and information about troop movements in the remote areas where guerrilla wars are fought.

If you don't like the way we give away land, we'll give away your family. You have five days to leave the country.

Death Squad notice to Luis Dominguez, El Salvador

Now the Army is requiring every family to be identified with its card and its photograph. The Army says that it is going to give each family a flag to put above its home, so when a helicopter or warplane comes to bomb, this flag will be the signal that the family is in agreement with the Army. We have seen that other people who have identified themselves, and already have their flags, but who are near where an attack is made, have been bombed by the Army anyway.

Village leader, Guatemala

We began to organize. Our organization had no name. We began by each of us trying to remember the tricks our ancestors used. They say they used to set traps in their houses, in the path of the *conquistadores*, the Spaniards. The first step the community took was to have my father, the village leader, living in the center of the community. All the members of the community, who lived some way off, could come down, and we'd live together or with our houses close together so that we could call to each other when the landowner's people came. This was the first step we took. We held a meeting and discussed it with everybody.

We began teaching our children to be discreet. They're usually discreet anyway, but we advised them not to say a single word to any children who weren't from our village about what their parents were doing. We performed a ceremony before beginning our self-defense measures. It was a village ceremony where we asked the Lord of the natural world, our one God, to help us and give us permission to use his creations of nature to defend ourselves with. The following day everyone came with ideas of how to defend themselves. Some brought stones, others machetes, other sticks, others their work tools. The women brought salt, hot water, etc. We put all our ideas together.

Civilians and their property are the primary targets of the Army in guerrilla warfare. *Near right::* Army forces sweep through a Salvadoran village, randomly killing civilians. *Far right:* a home near Palo Grande, El Salvador, is devastated when the Army occupies the village. The conflict in El Salvador has driven more than one million persons from their homes.

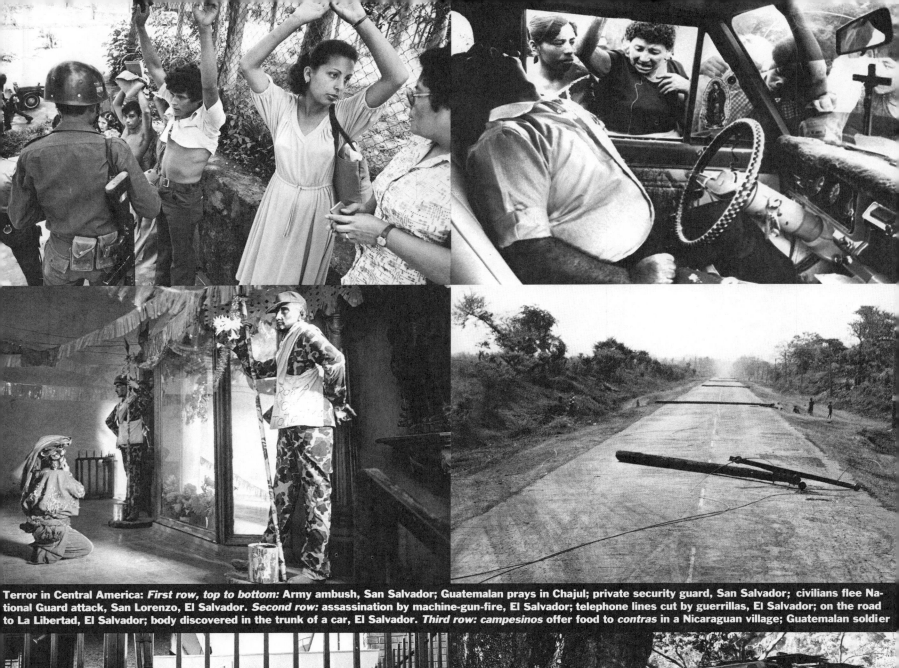

Terror in Central America: *First row, top to bottom:* Army ambush, San Salvador; Guatemalan prays in Chajul; private security guard, San Salvador; civilians flee National Guard attack, San Lorenzo, El Salvador. *Second row:* assassination by machine-gun-fire, El Salvador; telephone lines cut by guerrillas, El Salvador; on the road to La Libertad, El Salvador; body discovered in the trunk of a car, El Salvador. *Third row: campesinos* offer food to *contras* in a Nicaraguan village; Guatemalan soldier

fraternizes with Indian girl, Nabaj, Quiché; National policeman uses ice cream vendor as shield during skirmish, San Salvador; interrogation of villagers, El Salvador. *Fourth row:* arrest for failure to carry identification card, El Salvador; tailor killed in crossfire between Army and guerrillas, El Salvador; market day, San Juan Cotzal, Guatemala; murdered American church workers, San Salvador.

We started developing our security system, and each member of the community had special duties to carry out. The children, the women, the young people, the adults, and even the old people had their roles to play. Our animals, especially the dogs, helped us with defenses too.

When people were least expecting it, we'd cause some confusion in the village to see how we'd react. We tested our traps and our emergency exits. We realized that when the Army arrived, it wouldn't be very sensible to escape into the mountains in single file along the paths. So we dug large ditches and underground paths. Whenever a village leader gave the signal, we'd all gather in one place. We broke with many of our cultural procedures by doing this, but we knew it was the way to save ourselves.

RIGOBERTA MENCHU,
Indian leader, Guatemala

If we speak out, they kill us. If we're suspected of speaking out, they disappear us. And if we keep our mouths shut, they think we're hiding something. So they kill us for that too.

MANLIO ARGUETA, writer, El Salvador

Civil patrol members *(right)* line the road at dawn near Nebaj, Guatemala. Some 600,000 males, sixteen to sixty years of age, are required to serve without pay for twelve or twenty-four hours every seven to fourteen days, depending on where they live. Officially, the patrol guards citizens against guerrilla attack, but the Army, which created the civil patrol in 1981, uses the men to monitor activities and movement of peasants. *Below:* A flag-raising ceremony begins every day in Tzalbal model village, Guatemala. Forced from their land and resettled in government-built, Army-controlled communities beginning in mid-1983, some 70,000 Guatemalans are confined in the country's thirty-two model villages.

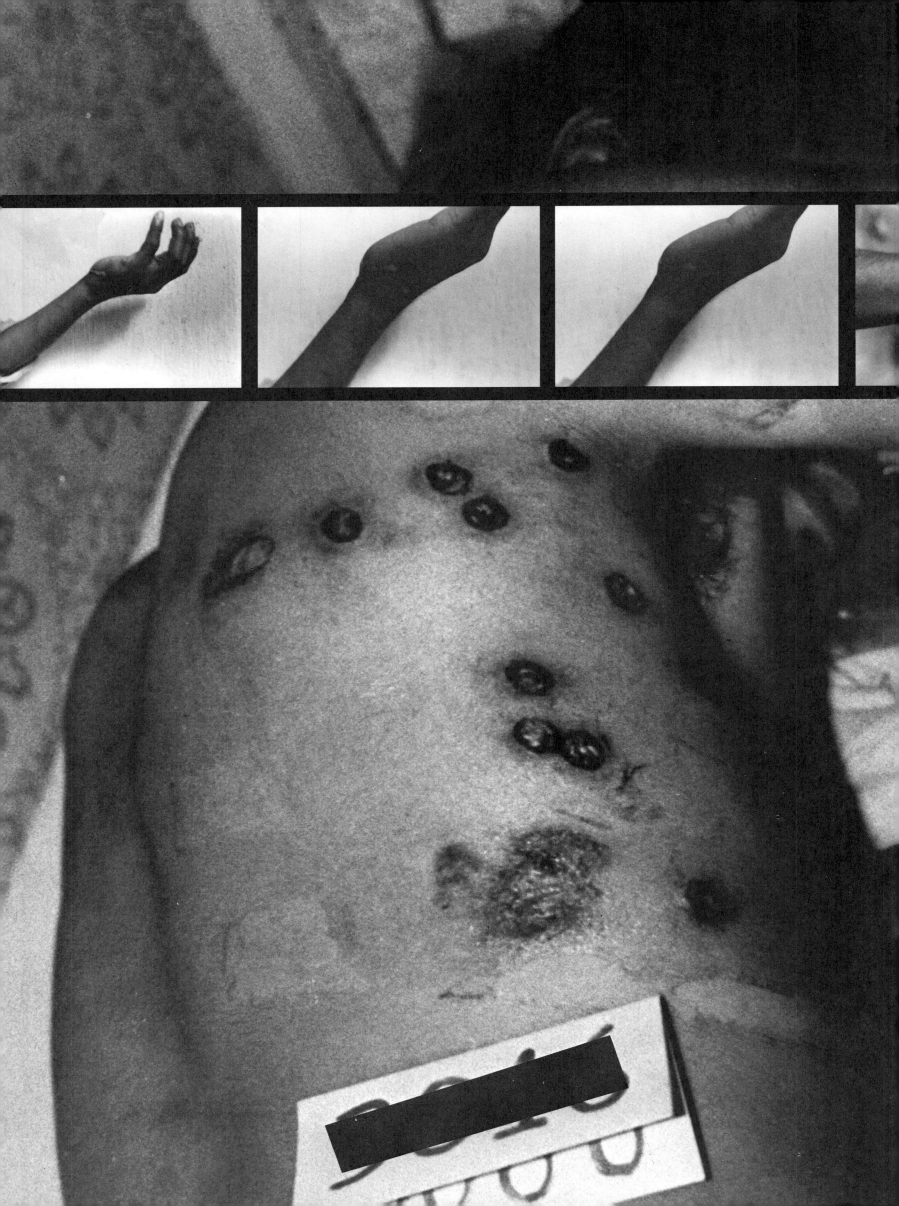

THE TORTURE MACHINE: WHAT IS EFFICIENT IS GOOD

severe and prolonged beating

amputation of digits, ears, nose

application of thumb screws or other compressive instruments

planton: victim, often hooded and forced to stand in one position for hours or days, sometimes with outstretched hands or while holding weights

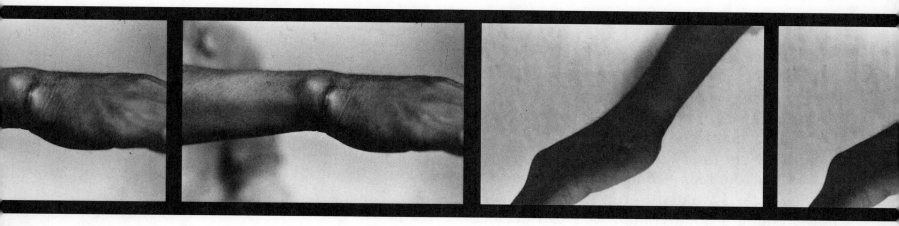

picana electrica: victim tied with wet strips of cloth to metal bed or bed spring and shocked by electrodes attached to wrists, ankles, or genitals

wet submarine: victim's head submerged in tank of water, often filled with vomit, blood, urine, or feces, and held down until near asphyxiation

dry submarine: victim's head covered with plastic bag, often filled with noxious substances, preventing him from breathing

potro: victim's ankles and wrists tied to modified bed frame or table and simultaneously stretched

burns of the skin: victim burned with cigarettes, fire, caustic substances, or electric current

la bandera: hooded victim hung by the wrists so he is unable to touch floor

parrots perch: victim suspended head down from horizontal pole placed under the knees, with wrists bound to ankles

sexual torture: victim raped homosexually or, if female, by one or more men. Foreign bodies inserted into vagina or anus and twisted to cause painful tearing of tissue

telephono: forceful and repeated blows with cupped hands to the external part of the ear

apollo: victim's head covered with metal hood to amplify the screams

diagnosis of mental illness: victim labeled as schizophrenic, paranoic, or schizoid and committed to mental wards for "treatment"

falanga: victim tied to a bench while soles of his feet beaten with a cane, stick, or other wooden tool

el caballete: victim, hooded and handcuffed, forced to straddle violently moving iron bar suspended in mid-air

black slave: electrical apparatus that inserts heated metal skewer into victim's anus

cachots noirs: cells totally devoid of light

el quirofano: victim forced to lie on table for extended period of time, with upper portion of body unsupported

le petit déjeuner: victim made to drink own urine

le déjeuner: victim beaten systematically on the shoulders

le rodeo: victim forced to run or crawl carrying heavy weight until exhausted

cajones: prolonged confinement in a box or other restricted space

bastani murghi: victim's nose and neck bound with tight cord, forcing head back and causing intense pressure on bridge of nose

stones thrown at testicles

deprivation of food, water, sleep

excrement in food

pharmacologic manipulation: victim given sodium pentothal, haloperidol, or chlorpromazine to cause confusion, disorientation, or tremors

insulin injections to cause seizures

Who tortures? Five sadists, ten morons, fifteen clinical cases? Respectable heads of families torture. The officers put in their hours of work and then go home to watch television with their children. What is efficient is good, the machine teaches. Torture is efficient: it extracts information, breaks consciences, spreads fear. It is born, and it develops the complicity of a black mass. He who doesn't torture will be tortured. The machine accepts neither innocents nor witnesses. Who refuses? Who can keep his hands clean? The little gear vomits the first time. The second time it grits its teeth. The third time it becomes accustomed and does its duty. Time passes, and the gear's little wheel speaks the language of the machine: hood, electric prod, submarine, stock, sawhorse. The machine requires discipline. The most talented end up taking a liking to it.

EDUARDO GALEANO, writer, Uruguay

A Chilean victim scarred by rubber bullets *(left)* is photographed in Santiago. Tens of thousands of Chileans have been tortured since the military coup by General Augusto Pinochet in 1973. Amnesty International estimates that more than one-third of the world's governments routinely torture their citizens—men, women, and children—to extract information about political activities. *Above:* a Guatemalan man rotates his mangled arm, pummeled by repeated beatings during his interrogation.

The soldiers came on December 11. They separated everyone—men in one place, women in another, and the children by themselves, and then they locked us all up. First they took the men outside and shot them. Next it was the women's turn.

When I heard the shots, I just fell. I wasn't shot, but I pretended to be. While the soldiers began dragging bodies away for burning, I crawled away. I made it to the brush.

I was in anguish because my kids were locked up. Then the soldiers started killing them. They cut their throats and choked them. I could hear the kids yelling, "Mama, they're stabbing me!" I wanted to run to them, but I knew I couldn't do anything. And so I decided to stay alive so I could serve as a witness to that crime.

When I returned, there were just little bones left. I couldn't recognize any sign of my kids, but I found part of my husband's maroon shirt.

RUFINA, forty-year-old woman, El Salvador

Twenty days ago masked men stopped a bus full of people on the mountain road at dawn and forced everyone off the bus, telling them to drop their pants and "touching" the women. But they didn't rob us, which is all the guerrillas do, so we believe it was the Army out to frighten and humiliate us.

Widows in a model village, Guatemala

All men, sometimes as young as ten years of age, must join the *Patrulla de Autodefensa Civil* [Civil Patrol]. They call it "self-defense." It's very ironic. If a man refuses to join, then the Army shoots him and says he is a subversive. We have to go out once a week for twenty-four hours. We receive no pay, which is a hardship for us, because we are now in bad times. In our group there are six. Three of us are given guns. We walk around the countryside of our hamlet in pairs. If we see anybody walking around,

In Buenos Aires *(right)* citizens commemorate the *"desaparecidos"* with paper silhouettes inscribed with the names of Argentineans who have been "disappeared" by death squads or the Army. Some 15,000 people, many abducted in broad daylight, were "disappeared" in Argentina from 1976 to 1978 at the height of General Jorge Rafael Videla's repressive regime. "Disappearing" people, as a strategy to terrorize the population, has been used in many countries of Latin America since the practice began in Guatemala in 1966. Not knowing whether a family member is dead or alive, relatives make the rounds of morgues in the hopes of ending their painful uncertainty.

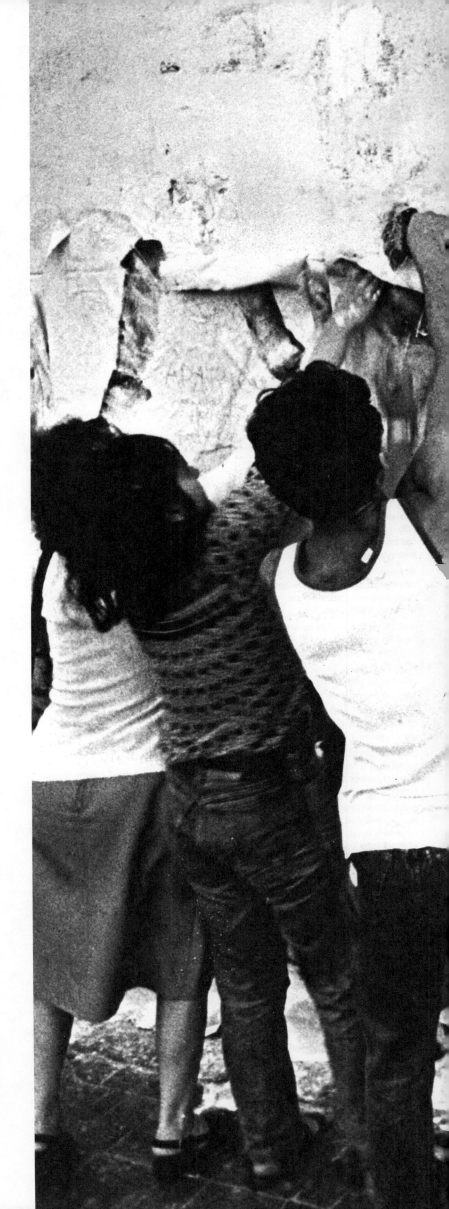

TAMANTE
DE
ANARAZ G.
27 años
9/4/77
Marinis
Lida
Beatriz
30 años
3/6/76
APA
CO

even people we know, we have to bring them to the Army base for interrogation. After 6 PM we have to shoot anyone we see.

Civil Patrol member, Guatemala

He was a student of economics at the university. He was going to work; he left the house at two o'clock in the afternoon, but then he was taken by a group of heavily armed men. We know this from a boy who works waxing cars at the university. He was there, and he told us. Since then we have denounced this to the police; we've looked for him in hospitals, in all the detention centers. We even went to the morgue to look for him, but we've had no news of him. Yesterday it was eleven months since my son "disappeared"; we've tried every means to locate him. He was the sole support of our house; he left a little one of nine months old. It's not possible they just "disappear" people like that. It's just as if the earth opened and swallowed them up.

Mother, Guatemala

When I was fourteen and graduated from primary school, my whole class joined or went to the military school or boot camp. Our job was to destroy whatsoever unknown person.

We didn't know what we would be doing when we joined. Most of us joined because we wanted to advance personally. In my case, I dreaded the thought of working by the machete—working on my family's parcel of land. It was too hard and too much suffering and poverty. I would do anything to avoid that.

There were approximately a thousand in my battalion—all about my age. About six-hundred of them had been kidnapped by soldiers. They were picked up in markets and forced into the Army. Most of them were very ignorant, illiterate. They didn't know what was happening.

After six months of training, we were divided up. About two hundred of us were sent to paratroopers school. We learned parachuting, self-defense, torture, and how to kill using a bayonet. I became a first sergeant as soon as we got there. I was smarter than the others and learned quickly and knew how to organize others.

The purpose of the torture and bayonet killing was to be able to kill and not leave traces that the military had done the killing. We learned how to break bones, puncture lungs, which made bodies inflate, rupture or sever blood vessels so they would bleed to death. We learned how to electrocute using two needles and an outlet. We used this especially against professors and students.

All but one of the two-hundred of us graduated, and we were sent to different military bases. I was sent with my group of forty-five to the *Zona Tacapa*. Our first assignment was to kill 1,500 *campesinos* from different zones in the area. We were given a list of names and told that these *campesinos* were buying and selling their produce through cooperatives, that they had refused to sell to the government corporation, ENDECA, from which the government made a lot of money. The other reason was simply that the *campesinos* were sitting on good land that either a military officer or a millionaire or the government wanted.

For children four and under, we cut off their heads. For those five and over, we killed them by beating but without leaving any external signs. We did this mostly to save ammunition. For those twelve and over, we tortured and also killed by beating. Some we put in a sack with insecticide called Gameźan. They would thrash about in the sack, and we would open it. They would come out half-crazy and choking. We would eventually kill them that way.

My group was then sent to Quiché in 1978, when General Lucas García was elected president. Our orders were to kill whole families. The reason why we killed is that we were told the Americans wanted more communists killed, and if we did that, we would get a salary increase, better food, new shoes, and new helicopters.

I remember one case where the owner of a coffee plantation had killed the wife of one of the *campesinos* who had six children. The owner then went to the man and gave him fifty *quetzales* to keep his mouth shut. One of the military police went and cut off the *campesino's* ear and six of his toes. One of my friends then killed the military policeman who did this and killed the peasant, because he was suffering and dying from the wounds. He put him out of his misery.

When my group arrived in Cotzal Quiché, we participated with five-hundred other military po-

Former member of a Guatemalan death squad.

"We participated with five-hundred other military police in a massacre of over five-hundred persons. We killed them in about twenty-five minutes. We were given lists, and then we killed."

lice in a massacre of over five hundred persons. We killed them in about twenty-five minutes. We were given lists, and then we killed. We didn't do any investigation, so there was no effort to convert the peasantry from their communism. My soldiers didn't know what communism was; they were uneducated. I cooperated because I did not want to go back to living by the machete on the farm.

We killed whole families, because it was what the military wanted, so it was necessary not to leave any heirs. Frequently we went into a village posing as guerrillas and gave a talk. From a nearby private car, soldiers would notice who would cheer for us, and then other soldiers would come and grab the guerrilla-sympathizers and either kill them there or on the road.

I was in Quiché in 1978 and 1979 and then asked for a reduction in rank. I thought that the orders I was receiving were bad, stupid. I wanted to try to convince the *campesinos* to change. I didn't think what we were ordered to do made sense. The reasons they gave I no longer accepted. I was now smarter than those giving me orders. I was married at this time, and my wife really didn't believe that I was doing what I told her I was doing.

In late 1979 I was moved to another branch, the *Policia Judicial,* which is part of the military police as well. I was still in Quiché. On my very first shift, I was to receive seventeen heads from different patrols that had been sent out to kill *campesinos* and bring in their heads. They were put in bags and left in different parts of the city with notes on them using slogans from the different guerrilla groups. That was to give the impression that guerrillas did the killing. I remember that night, because the patrols came in and one man, trying to impress my chief with his machismo, threw a head on the chief's desk—blood all over the place.

My uncle, who was chief of patrols of the National Police, then offered me a chance for advancement if I would lead a massacre of the village where his wife's family lived and the one where my wife's family lived. I remember getting the list and seeing my mother-in-law's name on it. I decided I couldn't do it. I warned the family of my uncle's wife, but they didn't believe me. In fact they told my uncle, and he told my mother that he would find me, no matter what, and kill me. I told her not to worry. Later my uncle carried out his wish and massacred the whole family of his wife. I led the family of my wife and the other villagers to Mexico. My uncle bragged of having killed 3,500 persons all by himself.

Five months before this, my daughter was killed. She was eighteen months old. She was playing on the curb in front of our house. A car pulled up and men got out. They machine-gunned some men on the sidewalk, killing them. A stray bullet killed my daughter.

I remember one American who trained us in military school. One in my group would make fun of him for his broken Spanish. One day the American soldier got mad, took out his gun, and shot the soldier point blank. He made a

Rosario   January 6, 1898 (89)
Ramon Lopez   September 6, 1902 – November 11, 1981
Alejandrino Gomez   November 10, 1903 – May 22, 1981
Pedro Hernandez   August 15, 1903 – March 17, 1981
Mario Lopez   May 21, 1904 – November 11, 1981
Hernando Velasco   February 4, 1906 – July 1980
Coronado Hernandez   March 23, 1907 – December 17, 1980
Pedro Gomez   February 16, 1911 – April 6, 1981
Antonia Lopez   May 18, 1920 – March 17, 1981
Aquilino Lopez – June 5, 1921   (60)
Maura Lopez –   January 4, 1924 (57)
Guadalupe Lopez   August 23, 1929 – June 29, 1982
Rigoberto Gomez   October 15, 1938 – November 14, 1982
Teresa Hernandez   June 27, 1938 – August 6, 1980
Luis Lopez   May 4, 1952 (30)
Lazaro Gomez   March 10, 1949 – October 1981
Francisco Hernandez   July 3, 1953 – August 8, 1980
Domingo Velasco   September 12, 1959 – September 29, 1983
Aparecio Lopez   April 6, 1963 – January 30, 1981
Fidencio Hernandez   May 21, 1957 – February 27, 1980
Pilar Gomez   January 30, 1961 – January 18, 1983
Manuel Velasco   November 10, 1960 – August 1980
Demecio Hernandez   July 16, 1960 – February 27, 1980
Pedro Gomez   August 22, 1959 – February 27, 1980
Isabel Gomez   June 29, 1962 – August 1980
Regina Hernandez   February 6, 1962 – August 6, 1980
Pedro Velasco   July 14, 1964 – July 2, 1982
Ginaro Lopez   November 11, 1966 – February 12, 1983
Manuel Hernandez   July 10, 1967 – January 30, 1981
Mario Gomez   March 23, 1970 – October 1984
Francisco Lopez   August 29, 1972 (15)
Adonato Lopez   April 16, 1968 – June 29, 1982
Aranulo Gomez   July 23, 1968 – March 17, 1981
Carmela Lopez   November 16, 1984 (13)
Miriam Lopez   May 30, 1967 (8)
Aracela Lopez   February 16, 1978   (6)

An eighty-nine-year-old Salvadoran woman weeps as she recounts how twenty-eight members of her family were killed from 1980-81 by torture or in Army massacres.

hole in his chest and a massive hole in his neck.

I knew Ríos Montt, Lucas García, Arana Osorio. I ate with them, talked with them.

I now hear the cries of children when I am walking alone. I remember those I just blew to pieces.

Ex-Army sergeant, Guatemala

We found these soldiers and we took them to the ditch and made them assemble our friend again on the ground like a man and ask forgiveness of the corpse.

Labor leader, El Salvador

The planes were shooting at the houses and made the banana trees and bushes fall down. The flowers were blown over by the wind of the bombs. My father and my little sister were working this small plot of land. I was on my way to bring them *tortillas* with salt. The bomb killed my cousin who was also working there. We had chickens who were killed. The soldiers left us only one little chicken. The house near the well, where we went to get water, was burning. We were afraid of the bombs, my mama and me, and we ran away. The bombs uprooted the trees. When we could not live any longer in our village, we hid in this little gully, my mama, my papa, and I. But we caught malaria. In the past, we planted beans and corn, but they destroyed everything. Now, I have a big ulcer, because I was hungry so often.

ANA DE JESUS ERNADES,
twelve-year-old girl, El Salvador

Extermination plan: destroy the grass, pull up every last little living thing by the roots, sprinkle the earth with salt. Afterward, kill all memory of the grass. To colonize consciences, suppress them; to stress them, empty them of the past. Wipe out all testimony to the fact that in this land there ever existed anything other than silence, jails, and tombs.

EDUARDO GALEANO, writer, Uruguay

An army sweep through Mayaland, Guatemala, levels the highland village and anything that can support life, including livestock and crops. During the early 1980s, the scorched earth offensive in Guatemala—the objective of the counterinsurgency war—reached its height. Deprived of their homes, *campesinos* flee to the countryside to survive. Ultimately their choices narrow: to seek Army protection in camps and model villages or to flee their country.

A Guatemalan woman and child stand before the ruins of their home in Choatalun, Chimaltenango, one of the areas targeted by the Army for selective repression and large-scale massacres in the early 1980s. Some 100,000-200,000 Guatemalan highlands children are either fatherless, motherless, or orphans. Forty percent of the Guatemalan population consists of widows and children.

SOME FACTS YOU SHOULD KNOW: THE DESTRUCTION OF CENTRAL AMERICA

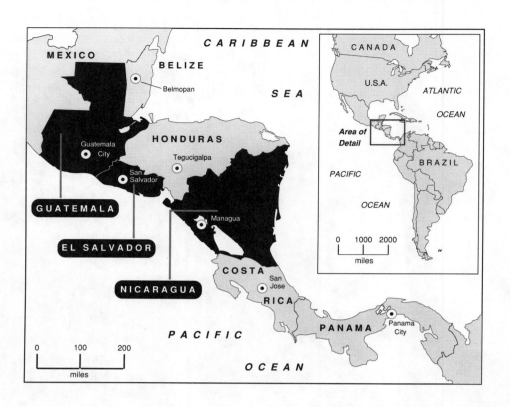

GUATEMALA

Population: 8.5 million

Life expectancy: 59 years

Percentage of population that is Indian: at least 60

Villages destroyed by army 1980—83: 440

Guatemalans killed by government forces 1966—86: 100,000

Guatemalans "disappeared": 38,000

Guatemalans internally displaced: 100,000 to 250,000

Children who lost one or more parents due to political violence 1980—85: 100,000—200,000

Number believed to have lost both parents: 30—40,000

Number of displaced at height of Army counterinsurgency campaign: 1 million

Number forced to relocate to militarized model villages since 1982: 50—75,000

Men, 16—60 years, forced to serve in civil patrols: 600,000

Guatemalan refugees living in the United States: 100,000

Number granted political asylum by U.S. Immigration and Naturalization Service 1983—86: 25

Percentage of applicants granted asylum: 1.7

EL SALVADOR

Population: 5.2 million

Life expectancy: 64.8 years

Principal cause of death among 15—24-year-olds: acts of violence, primarily military operations

Civilians murdered monthly by government forces and death squads at height of Army counterinsurgency campaign in 1980: 800

Civilians killed or "disappeared" by government forces or death squads 1981—87: at least 42,300

Executions by guerrillas 1984—87: 332

Civilians killed by mines or explosives, most believed to have been laid by guerrillas, 1985—87: 114

Men jailed for politically motivated offenses at Mariona prison, 1983—86: 2,165

Percentage of 1986 Mariona inmates who reported being physically tortured: 99.1.

Human rights monitors killed or disappeared 1980—87: 12

Military or police officers prosecuted for human rights abuses: 0

Villages bombed or strafed in 1986: 230

Salvadorans internally displaced by military operations since 1980: 525,000

Percentage of population: 10

Salvadorans currently displaced: 450,000

Percentage of Salvadoran population internally displaced or living in another country: 21.7

Average number of people in a displaced family: 7

Percentage of family members of displaced under 12 years: 40

Dollars spent in 1987 by United States to maintain displaced: $11.9 million

Percentage of Salvadoran children under five suffering from malnutrition: 27

Percentage of children of the displaced under five with malnutrition: 71

Physicians per inhabitant in El Salvador: 3.4 per 10,000

Salvadoran refugees living in Mexico and Central America: 181,000

Number receiving assistance from UNHCR: 29,161

Number accepted as political refugees by the U.S Immigration and Naturalization Service 1981—86: 869

Percentage of applicants granted asylum: 4.2

Salvadorans refugees, most undocumented, living in United States: 500,000

Amount Salvadorans in United States send to relatives in El Salvador each year: $350—450 million

United States aid to El Salvador 1980—87: more than $3 billion

Percentage of Salvadoran 1987 budget U.S. aid for the year represents: more than 50

Ratio of U.S. aid devoted to war and its effects, against amount devoted to reform and development: 3 to 1

Percentage of displaced who would like to return home: 70

Percentage who say they will return when war is over: 90

NICARAGUA

Population: 3.3 million

Population of Miskito, Sumu, and Rama Indians: 84—130,000

Life expectancy: 59.9 years

Number of Nicaraguan *cordobas* equal to one dollar in 1980: 28

Cordobas to the dollar in January 1988: 15,000

On the black market: 44,000

Percentage fall in real wages 1979—87: 94

Civilians wounded, kidnapped, or killed in conflict 1982—86: 9,638

Combatants wounded or killed: 29,576

Civilians killed by *contras* February—December 1987: 180

Health care workers killed, kidnapped, or wounded by *contras*: 84

Health facilities completely or partly destroyed: 65

Teachers killed by *contras*: 411

Schools destroyed or damaged: 67

Schools temporarily closed: 555

Students left without classrooms: 45,000

U.S. aid given or brokered for *contras*: $400—500 million

Miskitos, mostly civilian, murdered or "disappeared" by government forces: up to 100

Nicaraguans displaced in their country: 250,000

Percentage of population: 7.6

Number of Miskitos forcibly relocated by government in 1982: 8,500

Miskitos living as refugees in Honduras: 13,000

Percentage of Miskito population: 9—15

Nicaraguans who fled during the last years of the Anastasio Somoza regime: 127,500

Number who returned home: 112,000

Number displaced during last years of regime: 500,000

Number of Nicaraguans who fled Sandinista government immediately after Sandinista revolution: 20,000

Number of Nicaraguan refugees in 1987: 300,000

Percentage of population internally displaced or living outside Nicaragua as refugees: 16.7

Number granted political asylum by U.S. Immigration and Naturalization Service 1980—86: 3,724

Percent of those applying granted asylum: 21.6

DRAIN THE SEA, SCORCH THE EARTH: AN OUTLINE OF THE COUNTERINSURGENCY STRATEGY

ARYEH NEIER

Except for the prolonged and incredibly bloody war between Iran and Iraq, warfare in the 1980s means war between governments and their own people. The majority of the fourteen million refugees in the world today, who have been forced to flee for fear of persecution or death, are victims of insurgent and counterinsurgent strategies. Though not combatants themselves, their lives and livelihoods have been threatened because governments consider that they may suppress insurgencies more readily by driving people from their homes and, sometimes, because guerrilla forces believe that such actions will brighten their prospects. Most refugees are forced out because they have had the misfortune to live in contested territory and because they are considered expendable.

In our time not only the Central American nations of El Salvador, Guatemala, and Nicaragua have been plagued by such wars and suffer death, destruction, and dislocation, but also the South American nations of Colombia, Peru, and Suriname; in Africa such wars have taken heavy tolls in Angola, Chad, Ethiopia, Morocco, Mozambique, Namibia, Somalia, the Sudan, Uganda, and Zimbabwe, among others, and the war waiting to explode in South Africa repeatedly spills over into the neighboring "front line" states; in the Asian continent, Afghanistan, Burma, Cambodia, Indonesia, the Philippines, and Sri Lanka are among the countries suffering from such wars in this decade; in the Middle East, Iran and Iraq, who struggled against each other for eight years, continue to war against Kurdish independence movements, as does Turkey; the 1988 uprising in the Israeli-occupied territories verged on open warfare; and in Lebanon it sometimes seems as though everyone is at war with everyone else.

Ideology and ethnic identity are the main issues in this strife. Some ideological wars, such as those that have been fought in Afghanistan, Angola, and Nicaragua, have also involved efforts by the superpowers, relying largely on armies not composed of their own nationals, to assert hegemony beyond their own borders. Others, as in Peru and the Philippines, emerge out of long-standing grievances over land and the distribution of the nations's resources. At times ethnicity and ideology intertwine, as in the Eritrean guerrilla struggle against Ethiopian government forces, a war that has been waged for twenty-nine years; elsewhere, as in Sri Lanka, it is ethnicity alone that fuels conflict.

Internal wars are rarely characterized by pitched battles between contending armies. Instead, guerrillas and government troops struggle to "control" the civilian population in the countryside, where most such wars are fought. When they believe that peasants are aiding their enemies with food and information, armies may attack them to punish them or to force them to flee. It is easier to attack unarmed peasants than to confront their actual enemies directly. In this way armies attempt to deprive their enemies of the advantages of civilian support. Peasants are denied the right to remain neutral by insurgents who demand their livestock and their produce, or by "counterinsurgent" forces who destroy the food supply to starve the insurgents. The destruction of animals and crops may escalate into a strategy that relies on destroying the communities that produce the food. Peasants are terrorized, tortured, "disappeared," murdered, bombed, and strafed, and their crops are set on fire. To survive, their only alternative is to abandon their homes and communities, to live on the run or in squalid camps. In this way counterinsurgent warfare creates vast flows of displaced persons within countries and refugees who cross borders into neighboring countries.

Some trace the roots of contemporary counterinsurgent strategy to the 1890s and the practices of the British in combating the Boers in South Africa, the Spanish forces resisting the Cuban independence struggle, and United States forces confronting the Philippine independence movement led by Emilio Aguinaldo. In more recent times, however, it was Britain's success in the post-World War II era in defeating the communist guerrilla movement in Malaya that tested and proved the potency of counterinsurgency theories.

During World War II the principal resistance to the Japanese occupation of Malaya was mounted by communists, mainly Chinese. Following the war they continued to fight to create a communist state. In the battle against the communists the British forces under Sir Gerald Templer eschewed massive force and concentrated on depriving the guerrillas in rural areas of peasant support. The theoretician among Templer's staff officers was Robert Thompson, and it is with his name that counterinsurgency theory is particularly associated.

Thompson grasped the significance of Mao Zedong's dictum of the "long march" era that the guerrilla in the countryside is like a fish protected by a sea of peasants. As the image suggests, Mao found that long-suffering

Sir Robert Thompson (below, right), "father" of the counterinsurgency strategy, used the principles of China's Mao Zedong (left) in fighting communist guerrillas in Malaya in the 1940s.

Philippine Defense Secretary and future president Ramon Magsaysay *(left)* followed Thompson's advice in his government's struggle in the 1950s against the communist guerrillas known as the Huks. Members of the Philippine police display the head of a Huk *(above)*.

Chinese peasants provided a hospitable environment, nourishment, and concealment for his guerrilla forces. A generation later Thompson fought communist guerrillas in another Asian country by turning the sea against the fish through "civic action" programs in which land reform was promised, and by moving peasants into fortified compounds that were considered secure, that is, supportive of the government. The strategy succeeded. By 1953 or 1954 the insurgency had been defeated, the civilian death toll had been kept relatively low, and the economy had not been devastated.

As the insurgency in Malaya was being defeated, Thompson went on to the Philippines to advise Ramon Magsaysay, Defense Secretary and subsequently President, in his government's struggle against another guerrilla movement formed to fight against the Japanese occupation. The Hukbalahap—known as "Huks" to headline writers of the 1950s—also maintained their struggle after the war in an effort to create a communist state. Another adviser to Magsaysay was Colonel Edwin G. Lansdale of the U.S. Air Force who went to the Philippines on assignment for the C.I.A. Guided by Thompson and Lansdale, Magsaysay's forces implemented many of the same methods that had worked in Malaya and by 1954 they had achieved comparable success.

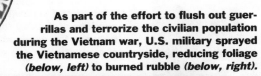

President John F. Kennedy *(left)*, impressed by the communist containment in Malaya and the Philippines, backed the use of counterterror to contain guerrilla warfare in Vietnam in the 1960s.

As part of the effort to flush out guerrillas and terrorize the civilian population during the Vietnam war, U.S. military sprayed the Vietnamese countryside, reducing foliage *(below, left)* to burned rubble *(below, right)*.

The successes in Malaya and the Philippines were considered models by the administration of President John F. Kennedy that took office in January 1961. The defeat of the French in Vietnam in 1954 and in Algeria later in the decade, the left-wing insurgencies in South Vietnam and Laos, and Fidel Castro's triumph in Cuba in 1959 all appeared to Kennedy to be part of a global grand design for a communist takeover. "Massive retaliation"—the Eisenhower-administration strategy that relied on the threat that the U.S. would use nuclear weapons to retaliate against an invasion of Western Europe by Soviet forces—was of no value in responding to communist guerrilla movements in the third world. To reduce the threat of nuclear war, Kennedy pressed successfully for a test-ban treaty and, at the same time, called on the Department of Defense and the C.I.A. to create the means to resist left-wing guerrilla movements by developing the United States's counterinsurgency capacity.

A guerrilla threat was particularly urgent in South Vietnam. Lansdale had been posted to Vietnam in 1956, where his exploits had earned him a thinly disguised portrait as Colonel Edwin B. Hillandale in William Lederer and Eugene Burdick's 1958 bestseller, *The Ugly American.* Thompson joined him in Vietnam and, in the new climate created by the Kennedy administration's determination to "draw the line" against communist guerrilla advances, became the architect of the "strategic hamlet" program. Hundreds of thousands of peasants were driven from their land by bombings, shellings, and forcible relocations in order to concentrate them in fortified villages. Though these were intended to be agriculturally self-sufficient settlements, great numbers of Vietnamese were forced into compounds where they had no means of sustaining themselves, increasing their misery and enhancing their sympathy for the communist insurgents.

The darkest side of the counterinsurgency program developed by the United States in the 1960s was "counterterror." In its most brutal form, counterterror was embodied in the C.I.A.- directed Phoenix Program in Vietnam in which villagers suspected of involvement in the Vietcong were systematically assassinated by agents of the Saigon government.

The C.I.A. and Pentagon architects of counterterror in Vietnam also sought to combat left-wing guerrilla movements elsewhere in the world. They were particularly alarmed by Fidel Castro's triumph by means of guerrilla

The success of Fidel Castro and his military advisor Che Guevara *(right)* in promoting communist insurgencies in Latin America in the 1960s led the U.S. to develop its counterterror capabilities as a method of halting revolutionary movements throughout the Western Hemisphere.

Trained in counterinsurgency techniques in the U.S., General José Efraín Ríos Montt *(above)* seized control of the government of Guatemala in a military coup in March, 1982, and used death squads and "disappearing" people, techniques originated in the 1960s, to eliminate opposition and to terrorize civilians. Assistant Secretary of State Thomas Enders *(above, right)* was an advocate of counterinsurgency in Latin America and a behind-the-scenes advisor to Central American leaders.

warfare in Cuba, by Castro's embrace of communism, and by the proclaimed intent of Castro and Che Guevara to aid and to organize guerrilla movements elsewhere in the hemisphere. To combat this threat President Kennedy launched the Alliance for Progress, an ambitious economic aid and development program. Without similar fanfare, however, officials of Kennedy's administration, and of the Johnson and Nixon administrations that followed it, also spurred the development of counterterror, helping to inaugurate the era of death squads and "disappearances" that began in Guatemala in 1966 and subsequently spread to other Latin American countries threatened by actual or potential attempts to replicate the Cuban revolution. Not all advocates of counterinsurgency approved of these developments, however. In a 1967 book, *Defeating Communist Insurgency,* Robert Thompson argued against counterterror, contending it would create more problems than it solved, and indeed would engender support for communist insurgents.

In the 1980s the assassinations of presumed guerrilla activists and sympathizers that characterized the counterterror programs developed in the 1960s have continued and

Counterinsurgency tactics have been used by governments of both the right and the left. In 1979, under orders of Soviet Premier Leonid Brezhnev *(below),* Soviet troops invaded Afghanistan *(bottom),* unleashing a scorched-earth policy meant to deprive guerrilla fighters of civilian support. At least three million butterfly bombs *(below)* were scattered throughout the countryside and maimed innocent villagers.

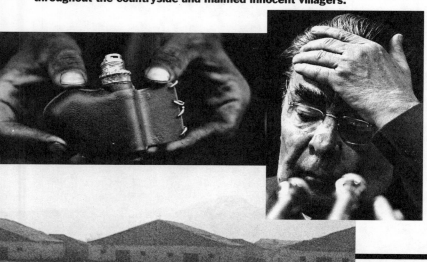

have been supplemented by regimes of every political persuasion. In Ethiopia Soviet-backed forces have imprisoned and tortured dissidents and bombed and shelled peasant sympathizers of anti-communist insurgent forces; in El Salvador and Guatemala U.S.-backed armies have massacred peasant sympathizers of communist guerrillas; in 1988 the U.S.-backed regime in Somalia massacred peasants in the northern part of the country as presumed supporters of Somali National Movement guerrillas; and in Sri Lanka, where ethnicity rather than political ideology is the driving force, every imaginable abuse has been committed. Millions have been terrorized, tortured, "disappeared," murdered, and imprisoned. Guerrilla forces in many lands have committed comparable barbarities. Bombings, strafings, and shellings by government forces and the landmines of guerrilla forces have killed and maimed great numbers, though this is often not their main purpose. The carnage is intended to drive people who wish to live at peace to abandon their homes and their fields; to deprive insurgent forces of a civilian population base; to make peasants into homeless wanderers in their own land, or refugees in the lands of others.

After World War II the nations of the world solemnly adopted declarations, treaties, conventions, and protocols to outlaw such cruelties. Yet four decades after the adoption of the Universal Declaration of Human Rights in 1948, and after the adoption of the Geneva Conventions in 1949 regulating the conduct of war, the barbarities that force people out of their homelands are more pervasive than ever.

Wracked by a civil war that has destroyed large areas of the countryside *(above)*, the Marxist government of Mozambique trains army recruits *(left)* to fight the Mozambique National Resistance, an anti-communist insurgency. Some two million Mozambican civilians have been forced from their homes.

In Ethiopia, the civil war between the Marxist government of President Mengistu Haile Mariam *(left)* and secessionist rebels *(right)* from Tigray and Eritrea provinces, has caused nearly two million civilians to abandon their homes.

Demanding independence from Sri Lanka, Tamil insurgents rioted in downtown Colombo in 1983, destroying sections of the city *(below)*. As a result of ethnic strife between the dominant Sinhalese and minority Tamil communities, nearly one million Sri Lankans, out of a population of fifteen million, have been internally displaced or have fled abroad.

FORBIDDEN FRONTIERS OF EASTERN EUROPE: WHEN GOVERNMENTS DECIDE WHO LEAVES

JERI LABER

Refugees from the Soviet Union and Eastern Europe are not driven from their countries by internal warfare or by the state-instigated counterinsurgency actions that destroy the homes of so many people in Central America, Africa, and other parts of the world. On the contrary, citizens of the Eastern bloc countries, especially those who want to seek refuge abroad, often cannot leave their countries, even when their lives become unbearable. They are confined behind closed borders; only their governments have the right to decide who leaves and who stays.

Most, though not all, who have made it to the West first faced the difficult personal decision to leave their homeland. More often than not they are people who, having achieved a certain economic, educational, or social level in society, came to reject a system that does not allow anyone to question the state's authority. They seek freedom—artistic, cultural, religious, intellectual—and in doing so embark on a journey that usually starts years before they actually cross their country's borders. It begins when they face the forbidden frontiers in their own minds, stepping outside the existing order and, ultimately, rejecting it. They risk their livelihood, their liberty, and sometimes even their lives.

Dissidents in the Eastern bloc countries—those who speak out against the actions of their governments—face a variety of punishments, depending on the will of the state. Only a small number have been banished abroad against their own wishes. Many more have ended up in prisons, or in psychiatric hospitals, or have been sent into internal exile, displaced in their own land. Others are subjected to constant persecution and harassment; their homes and cars are taken from them; their telephones are disconnected; their children are denied the opportunity for higher education. They are ostracized by society and forced to live within a tight circle of fellow dissidents, internal "refugees" in a hostile environment. Under such circumstances some decide to seek refuge abroad.

But many who apply for permission to leave have been refused. They have waited for years, growing old, disheartened, despairing. Some have tried to leave illegally, driven to acts of desperation—scaling the Berlin Wall or hijacking a jetliner. Some secretly nurse their desire to leave. They hope for an opportunity to travel abroad on official business and then to defect and seek political asylum.

Their governments are capricious. It is not unusual for exit visas to be denied to those who wish to leave, while those who wish to stay are sometimes forced out. Families are divided. Those who manage to leave, legally or illegally, have little hope of ever being allowed to cross back over the closed and closely guarded border.

The border that now divides Europe is a product of World War II. Stretching more than 4,000 miles, from Norway in the north to Turkey in the south, weaving an irregular, un-natural path through the center of Europe, it has sundered the integrity of the continent, separating "East" from "West." It is heavily fortified, as if to ward off an attacking army.

During Stalin's time, the "iron curtain" was tightly drawn, and the cultures of the two Europes were forced to go their separate ways. Even now, when contact between East and West is greater and more congenial than it has been in decades, the border remains immutable. It divides Germany in two and separates the "East"—the U.S.S.R., Poland, Czechoslovakia, Hungary, Romania, and Bulgaria—from Western neighbors such as Norway, Finland, Austria, Yugoslavia, Greece, and Turkey. It is illogical: Vienna, although considerably further east than Prague, remains in the "West"; it is only 100 kilometers from the Slovakian border, but the city seems light-years away from its sister cities of Prague and Budapest.

The border is delineated by parallel lines of barbed wire and electrified fencing. Watchtowers loom up at frequent intervals, and floodlights restlessly search the area throughout the night. There are relatively few places along the border where passage between East and West is permissible, and these checkpoints are blocked by iron barriers so thick and heavy no car can crash through. The customs inspectors are meticulous: they are on the lookout for ideas and people—the first to keep out, the second to keep in. They carefully inspect the obligatory visas. They pore through visitors' address books. They take away books and magazines. They inspect suitcases, turn car seats inside out, and slip large mirrors between the wheels of cars to make sure that no one is hiding there. These tight security measures are a strong deterrent to those who might otherwise seek to leave illegally.

Would-be émigrés from the communist world, Soviet Jews in particular, have become political pawns in a complex game that is being played by the superpowers. The United States, responding to domestic lobbying groups, presses the Soviet government to open its borders. The Soviets, in turn, grant visas arbitrarily, as a gesture aimed at increasing trade or other benefits from the West. The U.S. Congress in 1974 passed the Jackson-Vanik Amendment to the Trade Act, making it possible for the United States to withhold trade benefits from any country with restrictive emigration policies toward ethnic or religious groups. For a time Jewish emigration from the Soviet Union increased, reaching a high of more than 51,000 in 1979, but then it dwindled to a low of 914 in 1986, reflecting the increasing strain in U.S.-Soviet relations. Under Mikhail Gorbachev, however, relations between the two superpowers have improved. In 1987, 8,155 Jews were granted exit visas. In 1988 Jewish, Armenian, and German emigration figures continued to rise; it is estimated that 18,000 to 20,000 Jews will leave in 1988. In addition, some 40,000 Germans, 15,000 Armenians, and 3,000 Pentecostals are expected to leave in 1988.

New problems have arisen with this increase in emigration: a financial or bureaucratic inability on the part of the U.S. to process all the applications of those seeking refugee status, and an increasing sensitivity on the part of Israel to the fact that most Soviet Jews prefer to resettle in the United States and not in Israel. In 1988 the U.S. government took measures to slow down the flood of Armenians and others seeking U.S. refugee status.

Soviet Jews flee from anti-Semitism and religious repression, although the Soviet Union does not admit to such practices or recognize them as grounds for leaving the U.S.S.R. Instead all emigration from the Soviet Union is officially predicated on grounds of family reunification. Since January 1987, Jews have been restricted by the fact that those who wish to emigrate must have invitations from immediate family members abroad; these usually come from Israel, although some are from other countries. The Soviet Union in the fall of 1988 indicated that it might drop the requirement of an invitation from an immediate relative.

Most Soviet Jews, once they cross the border, choose to go to the United States instead of Israel, and they apply to the United States for refugee status. This preference has become a source of irritation and embarrassment, not only to Israel but to the Soviet government as well. It is difficult for Soviet leaders to claim that theirs is the better system when so many Soviet citizens wish to leave for the United States.

Aware of the political mileage it can gain in the superpower struggle, the United States has given preference to refugees from the Soviet Union and other communist countries and to people in Asia and Africa who are fleeing from communist oppression. Between 1980 and 1987, 52,122 Soviet émigrés and 545,567 Vietnamese, Laotians, and Cambodians were admitted to the United States as refugees or granted political asylum, while only 57 Haitians, 998 Salvadorans, and 32 Guatemalans received protection.

Although wounded Soviet pride may account, in part at least, for the tight controls the Soviets have imposed on those who wish to leave, the controls also underscore the government's concern about losing skilled labor and about a "brain drain" their economy can ill afford. Among those who have received asylum in the West are doctors, scientists, and other professionals. Some of the country's best thinkers and most creative talents have either defected or been banished from the U.S.S.R. and are now living and working abroad, including ballet stars Rudolph Nureyev and Mikhail Baryshnikov; musicians Mstislav Rostropovich and Vladimir Feltsman; and writers Alexander Solzhenitsyn, Vasily Aksyonov, and Joseph Brodsky. The government is now trying to woo some of them back.

Recently more people have been allowed to emigrate from the Soviet Union; former citizens have been allowed to return to visit or to resettle; and many Soviet citizens with relatives in the West have been allowed to visit them and to return home again. But elsewhere in Eastern Europe, especially in Czechoslovakia, Romania, and Bulgaria, restrictions remain severe. And the Soviet Union still has a long way to go before it can be said to observe the right to leave and return that was guaranteed by the 1975 Helsinki Final Act, signed by the Soviet Union and thirty-four other countries. If the Soviet Union and its Eastern bloc allies were to fulfill their obligations under the Helsinki accords and to open their borders so all might leave and return at will, they might find that fewer citizens would want to emigrate.

FORCED IN

Many Soviet Jews have been denied permission to leave their country because of their alleged knowledge of state secrets. Some 800 known cases of scientists are in this category. The definition of a "state secret" is arbitrary; it can include everything from matters affecting national security to those considered industrial secrets in the West. Moreover, despite promises by Mr. Gorbachev to change the policy, there is as yet no statute of limitations with regard to the possession of state secrets. Many would-be émigrés are denied visas because of jobs held twenty or more years ago, even though the information has long since been outdated. Some scientists who are denied permission to leave on grounds of possessing state secrets were, in fact, never exposed to sensitive material in their work. Others have been given no reason at all for years of consistent refusals.

Would-be émigrés live in a state of limbo, shunned by society and no longer able to find employment in their fields. In order to apply to emigrate, they are required to show not only a letter of invitation from a member of their immediate family abroad but also certificates from their place of work and from the house committee in the apartment complex in which they live.

MARK AZBEL Azbel, a scientist who was refused permission to leave the Soviet Union for many years before he was allowed to go to Israel, described the persecution: "No one wants to broadcast his intention of emigrating until he has to; but to obtain this certificate of residence is to announce your plans to hundreds of people, to everyone in your apartment building. Since it is known that an applicant may be kept waiting for months or years before his fate is decided—if it ever is—the prospect of this long-term notoriety is daunting."

SERGEI KHODOROVICH "I have no choice," said Tatyana Khodorovich when she was informed in 1987 that she and her family must emigrate in exchange for the release of her husband, human rights activist Sergei Khodorovich, who had been in prison for four years on charges of slandering the state. "These words are terrifying to me," Mrs. Khodorovich explained. "I never thought about leaving. Nobody in my family ever thought about leaving."

ANATOLY and GALINA KORYAGIN Dr. Anatoly Koryagin, who was arrested in 1981 for reporting on the practice of confining political dissenters in psychiatric institutions, was released from a labor camp on the condition that he and his family apply for exit visas to leave immediately. The Koryagins were stripped of their Soviet citizenship once they were abroad, without any possibility of appeal.

NAUM MEIMAN A mathematician, Meiman was permitted to leave the Soviet Union in February 1988, fourteen years after he began the application procedure for an exit visa. His work in classified mathematical calculation had ended in 1955. Meiman's human rights activities as a member of the Moscow Helsinki Group, combined with his desire to emigrate to Israel, made him a double target for vindictive authorities. For three years he fought for permission for his wife Inna to go the West for cancer treatment. She finally received approval in 1987, but he was not allowed to go with her. She died, alone, in Washington D.C. shortly after her arrival. Her husband was not allowed to attend the funeral. Meiman was seventy-six-years-old and ailing when permission to leave finally came in 1988. He now lives in Israel.

FORCED OUT

Given the large number of people who are seeking unsuccessfully to leave the Soviet Union, it seems ironic that the Soviet government has also expelled certain people who had no desire to leave their native land. Indeed, the government sometimes seemed to be taking malicious pleasure in forcing out those who most wanted to stay. For a Russian nationalist writer like Alexander Solzhenitsyn, who was put on a plane in February 1974 and banished from his homeland, separation from the Russian language and culture is a kind of spiritual death. Solzhenitsyn once wrote that a writer living in a repressive country is like a "second state," able to act as the conscience of society and to record its painful history. For this reason writers are often singled out by governments for unceremonious treatment.

Nor has the practice of forcible expulsion entirely ceased under Mr. Gorbachev. Just recently, this method provided a convenient way to resolve the embarrassing case of Paruir Ayrikyan, who was arrested in Yerevan in March 1988 on charges of "anti-Soviet slander." Ayrikyan, an outspoken Armenian nationalist, soon became the focus of an international protest. In July 1988 he was sent directly from jail against his will to Ethiopia. He ultimately found refuge in the United States.

MILAN KUNDERA Czechoslovakia is notorious for depriving its writers of citizenship. Kundera lost his citizenship in 1979 when his novel *The Book of Laughter and Forgetting* was published in France. His books have been removed from libraries in Czechoslovakia, and his plays have been banned from theaters. Other Czechoslovak writers, including Jiří Gruša and Pavel Kohout, also lost their citizenship while living abroad. Their fate serves as a warning to those who remain behind. Czechoslovak writers invited to go abroad to lecture routinely refuse such invitations, afraid that if they leave their country, they will not be allowed to return.

LEV KOPELEV Soviet writer Lev Kopelev had a premonition of his fate when he and his wife, Raissa Orlova, left the U.S.S.R. in 1980 to spend a year lecturing in Germany. Kopelev packed a handful of black Russian earth in a little box; he told the customs inspector he wanted it for his grave, should he happen to die while abroad. The inspector was not impressed. He did not allow Kopelev to bring the simple memento with him. When the Kopelevs lost their citizenship in 1981, while they were still in Germany, Orlova reported that they had "never felt so sad." Three of their four daughters, and many grandchildren, remain behind in the U.S.S.R.

JOSEPH BRODSKY Joseph Brodsky, writer and Nobel Prize Laureate, was condemned as a "parasite" and spent five years in exile in the U.S.S.R. He was forced to leave in 1972 and subsequently lost his citizenship.

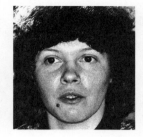

IRINA RATUSHINSKYA A gifted young poet, Irina Ratushinskaya was imprisoned for five years on charges of anti-Soviet propaganda. She was allowed to go abroad in 1987 for medical reasons, only to be stripped of her citizenship for "defaming the Soviet Union."

ACTS OF DESPERATION

Many citizens, frustrated in their attempts to leave Eastern bloc countries legally, have been driven to acts of desperation to find refuge abroad. Once their wish to leave becomes known, they become objects of suspicion, considered traitors by many of their colleagues and associates. Under such circumstances it is no wonder they are willing to take considerable risks to change their situation.

According to the West Berlin police, by 1986, twenty-five years after the Berlin Wall was erected, some 5,000 East Berliners had made it safely over, through, or under the Wall. But seventy-three people were known to have died trying to escape.

One of the more spectacular escapes occurred before dawn on September 16, 1979, when two East German families flew twenty-eight miles across the border in a hot-air balloon made from pieces of sheeting and nylon they had sewn together by hand. The four children and four adults balanced themselves on a six-foot-square iron platform attached to the balloon. Two were slightly injured in the landing.

RUDOLF NUREYEV and **MIKHAIL BARYSHNIKOV** Nureyev and Baryshnikov are probably the most famous of the many Soviet ballet stars who have defected to the West. Nureyev, a principal dancer in the Kirov Ballet Company of Leningrad, was only twenty-three when he left his troupe during a tour in Paris in 1961. Baryshnikov, also a leading dancer with the Kirov, left at the age of twenty-six while he was touring in Toronto in 1974. Baryshnikov asserted that his was an artistic, not a political, decision. "My life is my art," he declared. Both Nureyev and Baryshnikov have transformed their art since arriving in the West; they have also made a tremendous contribution to the art of American ballet.

EDWARD KUZNETSOV In 1970 a thirty-one-year-old, half-Jewish Soviet citizen, Edward Kuznetsov, frustrated in his efforts to emigrate legally, led a desperate plot to hijack a Soviet passenger plane and fly it over the border to Sweden. The conspirators never got near the plane; instead the group was arrested, and Kuznetsov was tried and sentenced to death. A worldwide protest led to the commutation of his death sentence to fifteen years of imprisonment. Kuznetsov served nine years before he was released in 1979 in a U.S.-Soviet prisoner exchange. He now lives in Munich.

THE WARRING WORLD: A TALLY OF CONFLICT AROUND THE GLOBE

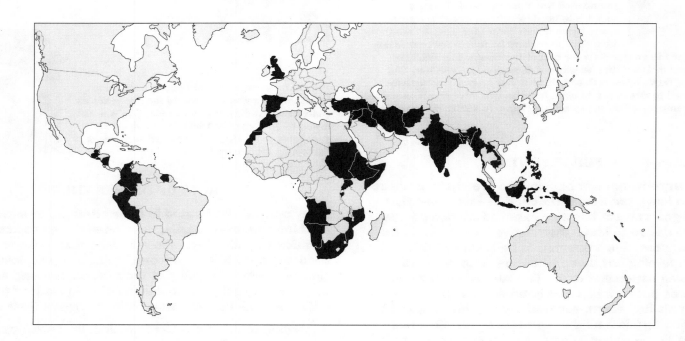

The 40-odd wars being fought today are primarily between state governments and political or ethnic groups that oppose the state government in power. Conflicts occur in every region of the world (darker areas); these are the wars that produce most of today's refugees.

LATIN AMERICA

El Salvador	FMLN
Nicaragua	Nicaraguan Resistance (truce)
Guatemala	URNG
Colombia	M-19, ELN, EPL and FARC (uneasy truce)
Peru	Sendero Luminoso
Suriname	Brunswijk insurgency

AFRICA

Angola	UNITA
Sudan	SPLA
Ethiopia	Eritrean and Tigrayan independence groups
Somalia	Somali National Movement
Uganda	numerous tribal and ideological groups
Burundi	flairups between Hutus and Tutsis
South Africa	ANC
Mozambique	Renamo
Namibia	SWAPO
Morocco	Polisario Front

EUROPE

Spain	ETA
Britain	IRA
Turkey	Kurdish independence groups

MIDDLE EAST

Syria	Israel, PLO
Israel	PLO
Lebanon	Shiite Moslems, Maronite Christians, Druze, Sunnis, PLO, and others

SOUTHWEST ASIA

Iran	Kurdish independence groups
Iraq	Kurdish independence groups
Afghanistan/ Soviet Union	*mujahedin*

SOUTH ASIA

India	Kalistan (Sikhs)
Sri Lanka	Tamil Eelam (Tamils)
Bangladesh	numerous tribal groups

SOUTHEAST ASIA

Burma	Karen and other groups
Cambodia/ Vietnam	Khmer Rouge and other groups
Laos	Hmong
Indonesia	East Timor, Irian Jaya
Philippines	NPA, MNLF

PACIFIC

New Caledonia/ France	Kanaki (FLNKS)

ARMS SUPPLIERS TO THE THIRD WORLD

		Value (1983—86 sales)	Change from 1979—82 to 1983—86
1.	Soviet Union	$59.8 billion	8.4%
2.	United States	$25.5 billion	1.4%
3.	France	$16.5 billion	42.1%
4.	China	$ 5.3 billion	157.7%
5.	West Germany	$ 4.0 billion	18.2%
6.	Britain	$ 3.4 billion	−49.4%
7.	Italy	$ 3.2 billion	−5.4%
8.	Czechoslovakia	$ 2.6 billion	130.0%
9.	Spain	$ 2.1 billion	162.2%
10.	Brazil	$ 1.2 billion	6.5%

TEN WEAPONS THAT TRAVEL THE WORLD

AK-47 assault rifle (Kalashnikov)
Manufacturers: U.S.S.R., China, Finland, East Germany,
Hungary, North Korea, Poland, Romania, Yugoslavia

M16 rifle
Manufacturer: U.S.

G3 Heckler and Koch rifle
Manufacturer: West Germany

FAL rifle
Manufacturer: Belgium

RPG-7 portable rocket launcher
Manufacturer: U.S.S.R.

SA-7 surface-to-air missile
Manufacturer: U.S.S.R.

M60 machine gun
Manufacturer: U.S.

RPK light machine gun
Manufacturer: U.S.S.R.

DSh K-38 heavy machine gun
Manufacturer: U.S.S.R.

HK 13 Heckler and Koch light machine gun
Manufacturer: West Germany

MILITARY SPENDING

WHO SELLS

	(Millions)
Soviet Union	$15,300
United States	12,300
France	4,600
Czechoslovakia	1,400
Poland	1,100
Italy	975
United Kingdom	825
Germany, West	625
China	575
Germany, East	550
Spain	500
Bulgaria	470
Romania	430
Yugoslavia	400
Korea, North	380
Brazil	330
Sweden	330
Israel	250
Hungary	240
Portugal	210
Belgium	200
Switzerland	200
Canada	190
Austria	160
Australia	120
Korea, South	100
Turkey	100
Japan	90
Libya	90
Egypt	70
Argentina	60
South Africa	50
Netherlands	30
Pakistan	30
Chile	20
Singapore	20
Vietnam	20
India	5
Indonesia	5

WHO BUYS

Iraq	4,000
Saudi Arabia	3,700
India	2,300
Cuba	2,100
Germany, West	1,700
Iran	1,700
Libya	1,600
Syria	1,500
Egypt	1,400
Soviet Union	1,100
Vietnam	1,100
Israel	1,000
Japan	1,000
Australia	925
Germany, East	825
Ethiopia	800
Angola	775
Poland	700
Bulgaria	675
United Kingdom	675
Jordan	625
Czechoslovakia	600
United States	600
Taiwan	575
Afghanistan	525
Venezuela	490
Pakistan	480
Malaysia	470
Algeria	460
Korea, South	430
Netherlands	430
Turkey	420
Yemen (Aden)	390
Korea, North	360
Tunisia	340
Nigeria	320
Belgium	310
Kuwait	300
Greece	290
Cambodia	280
China	280
Mozambique	270
Nicaragua	270
Norway	260
Italy	230
Yemen (Sanaa)	220
Switzerland	200
Argentina	180
Portugal	170
Thailand	160
Spain	150
Finland	140
Gabon	140
France	130
Morocco	110
Laos	100
Oman	100
Singapore	100
Canada	90
Denmark	90
El Salvador	90
Indonesia	80
New Zealand	80
Sweden	80
Un. Arab Emir.	80
Hungary	70
Peru	70
Guinea	60
Bangladesh	50
Brazil	50
Tanzania	50
Lebanon	40
Mali	40
Quatar	40
Sudan	40
Burma	30
Cameroon	30
Congo	30
Guatemala	30
Madagascar	30
Mexico	30
Philippines	30
Romania	30
Somalia	30
Sri Lanka	30
Yugoslavia	30
Austria	20
Burkina Faso	20
Chile	20
Costa Rica	20
Ecuador	20
Haiti	20
Honduras	20
Ivory Coast	20
Zaire	20
Bahrain	10
Benin	10
Chad	10
Colombia	10
Gambia, The	10
Guinea-Bassau	10
Guyana	10
Ireland	10
Liberia	10
Panama	10
Pap. New Guin.	10
Paraguay	10
Zambia	10
Botswana	5
Burundi	5
Cyprus	5
Dominican Rep.	5
Jamaica	5
Kenya	5
Malawi	5

An Ethiopian flees Welo province in search of food and protection from a civil war that has lasted twenty-seven years. Controlling the distribution of relief supplies in Africa becomes a political act, where in Ethiopia alone, one million people died from starvation in the 1984-85 famine. Among displaced people throughout the world, the decision to seek protection in a neighboring region or country comes only after repeated threats to one's survival.

IN
SEARCH
OF
REFUGE

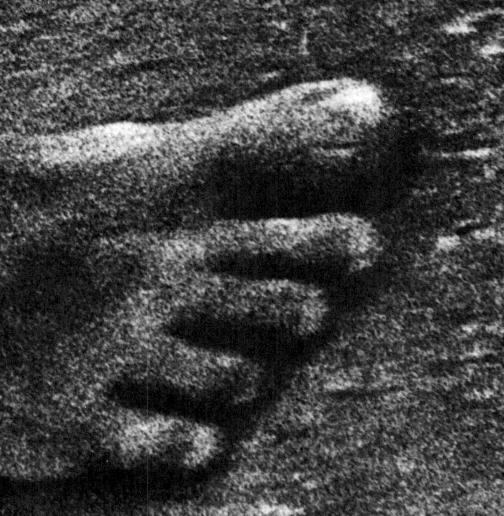

I remember the dawn of July 17, when we heard the cry, "Run, the soldiers are coming!" The children began to cry, terrorized, but after we started walking they calmed down some. Each person carried his belongings, his poncho, some *tortillas,* corn meal, or whatever he could find. Each child who could walk also carried something.

The people of three villages came together in one place. We were resting when we again heard shots nearby. Once again we fled. Finally we came to another place farther away, where we found more people from other villages.

A tank ditch marks the border between Thailand and Cambodia.

There we rested again and shared what we had. We ran out of water and ate dry corn meal. We became nauseated from lack of water. There were too many of us, so we decided to divide up into smaller groups. But in all this activity, families got divided up. In my group there was a child carrying his mother's clothes and a poncho, while his mother went off in a second group carrying their *tortillas.* Her oldest child was in a third group, and the father, with the rest of the ponchos, went with yet a fourth group. I saw a little girl about five years old who had lost her parents. But there we were!

We found a little orange tree loaded with oranges. We picked them all. They were very acidic, but they helped a lot. After a long walk—all day long—we came to another place about 9 PM and slept there. At this place they gave us hot *tortillas,* water, and a little salt.

On July 18 at 5 AM, we were all up and ready to go. We washed with the dew from the plants. We found yucca and some other food, and we each ate a little. We were busy doing

Forced to flee: Nicaraguan mother

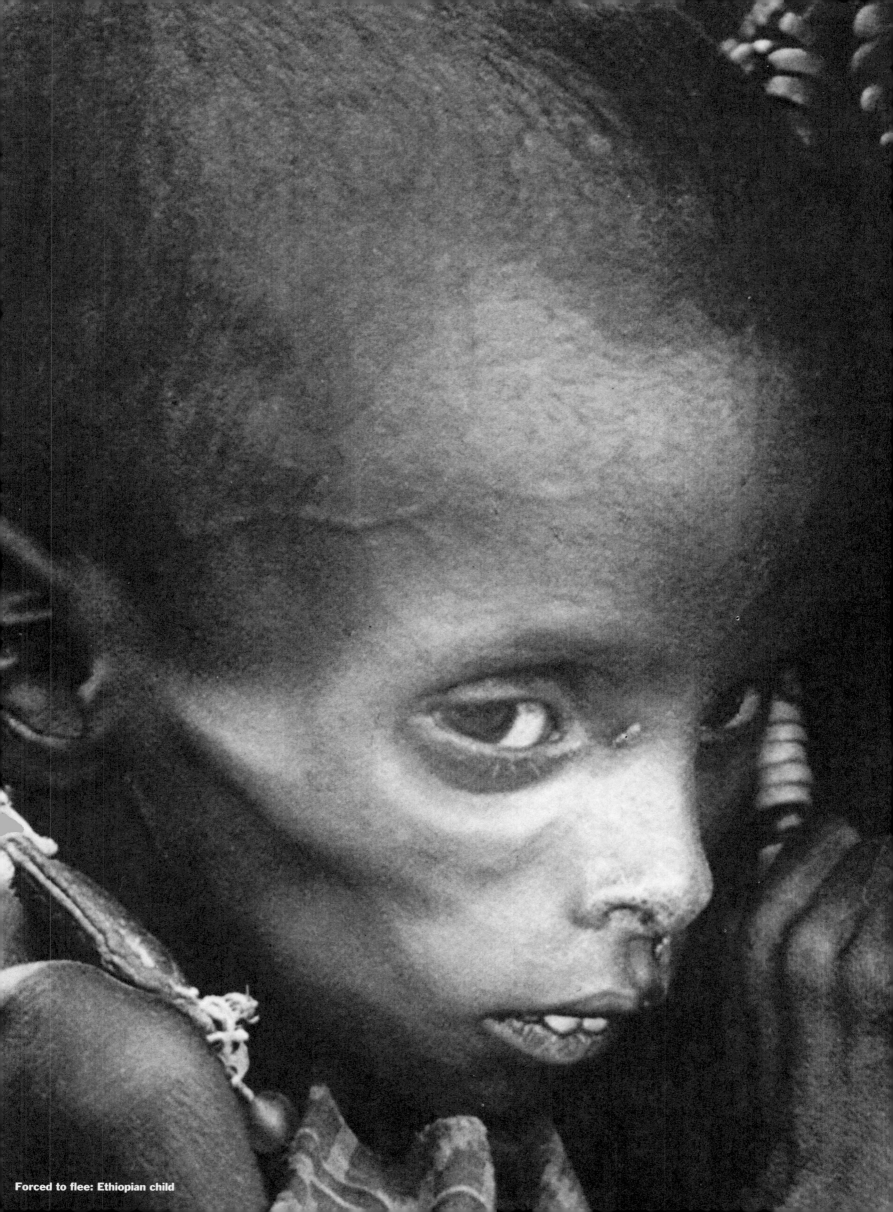

Forced to flee: Ethiopian child

"A man asked who could speak English. It was quiet. It was dark. He told us to be silent or we would be shot. We held our breath. There wasn't a sound on that crowded bus."

all this when we heard shots. We had to run again. Minutes later we saw the soldiers come running down a road. What hurt me most was seeing the old people with their canes, but thank God we managed to get away. From a distance, we saw the village burn.

REGINA HERNANDEZ, *campesina,*
Guatemala

We could bring only what fit into one small bag. They warned us not to take too much. For days I burnt documents on my terrace, papers from when I worked for my government, papers from when I worked for the Americans. I couldn't think, except to destroy whatever would bring trouble. I burnt photographs of the whole family at Tet, year after year, all of us together—my father's nine birds. I stared at the black-and-white pictures: me—tiny, smiling, a pigtail on both sides, holding my eldest brother's hand. Me, the angel in the school play, a tiara on my head. Me in China at the bottom of Sea Mountain, my children standing beside me.

As the pile of ashes floated away, I felt I was burning my life.

TRAN THI NGA, bookkeeper, South Vietnam

I left before my harvest. They would have taken it anyway.

Farmer, Ethiopia

We made lists. That was the manifest: name, sex, age. When the captain came for us, we went quickly to the bus, squeezed into the front with all our luggage on one seat as he had told us to. A man asked who could speak English. It was quiet. It was dark. He told us to be silent or we would be shot. We held our breath. There wasn't a sound on that crowded bus.

As we approached, the plane made a huge noise, like a C-130. It opened at the back, a mouth. We were thrown in like packets. The pilot ordered *stop* just as the last of our group

was in. Hundreds of us sat on the floor, a huge string tied around us, our babies on our laps. Many were sick.

We arrived at Clark Field, Philippines, at 1:30 AM. Everyone was quiet. We were handed medicine, blankets, mattresses. People were everywhere. There was much red tape: name, sex, age.

TRAN THI NGA, bookkeeper, South Vietnam

I was a shopkeeper at Ajunami, east of Mozo. The U.N.L.A. came and looted my shop. They were ten who came in the morning and kept shooting as they drew nearer to the door. In seeing this, we ran away leaving everything in the shop. After two days, I came back and found nothing at all. I then decided to move away because the whole roof of my grass house was burnt down by explosives. In it I found an old sauce pan that I carried with me as the only utensil from home. It has bullet marks on it, too!

Shopkeeper, Uganda

We were there in the house when we heard something like a bomb explosion. Then we saw a child who fell terribly wounded. She was just an infant, about a month old. We really got scared at that point; so we decided to leave, to run away. We set out by foot, and when it grew dark, we kept on walking. Finally, we got to a shelter where we stopped to rest. I don't recall the time when soldiers fell upon us. I stepped out of the shelter with my children when we heard the shooting. My children ran away from me, I guess because they were scared. I realized then that I had lost my children. This is one of my worries. I don't have my three children anymore; and they are a part of my body.

Mother, El Salvador

There were a hundred people in the group that came out of the village and seven from our family, including this child. There was snow

Forced to flee: Ethiopian farmer

Forced to flee: Vietnamese grandmother

and there was ice. Many had their feet frozen from frostbite. No water—our children's tongues were swollen from lack of water. It took us two weeks. The Russians bombed us all the way. They dive-bombed us day and night. This girl was on a horse with a baby under her arm. The Russian airplane came low, and she felt blood running. It was from the baby. She fell off the horse. The baby was dead. Of the hundred who left with us, only ten got through the mountain to Pakistan.

Woman, Afghanistan

On April 25 it all came to a head. They attacked from the north and east with heavy cannons and machine guns. Everyone left their homes and fled to the Old City on the seashore. Some desperately tried to put their families and possessions into the small fishing boats, but the sea was stormy and they were thrown back onto the shore. Everyone was wailing and weeping, and there was total chaos. My brother and I ran all over town trying to find a truck, but there weren't any. They were all either full of people or burnt out. There were many dead donkeys, too, with their trailers still attached to them, lying in the road. Next we went to the sea, but clearly there was no chance of escape there. In the end, we found a truck, and our family with three others climbed on. We had one suitcase with us; everything else we left at home. It took us seven hours to get to Majdal, where we slept the night. Early next morning we traveled on to Gaza. There we were: us and a suitcase.

Fayez, Palestinian

I packed up a few documents and some food and clothing. I felt very terribly sorry to leave, for I was abandoning half my life—all the assets, all that I had accumulated over the years of living and working in that town. I could not control my emotions at that time, and I burst into tears. I knelt down in front of the photographs of my dead parents, which hung above the dining table. I knelt down before their faces to pray, as I turned away from that life. And then I dragged my feet, and walked reluctantly from my home, and drove away from Pleiku.

SUN-JEN, businessman, South Vietnam

On the way, we met the soldiers again. We had a bit of our property, forty-five head of cattle. Our brother who had his ears cut was so powerless, he could not run fast enough because of the tortures he had received. He was recaptured and shot. Immediately we threw down our luggage and ran without anything. We had to carry the small children on our backs. On our way, bombs followed us. Many were victims as some of the bombs exploded either in front, behind, or sideways. Victims were left, and we proceeded. Almost nobody cared for the other. Children were lost and in critical condition; women even threw their children away so that they could escape.

Farmer, Uganda

My last days in the Soviet Union remain a chaotic blur in my mind's eye. I never slept more than two or three hours out of the twenty-four. Throughout all the years of refusal, I had always promised myself, and had persuaded Lucia to promise, that if our permission ever came, we would not risk waiting an extra hour. We had suffered so much anguish on behalf of friends who delayed—it was only too easy to be trapped again in the interval when one was no longer a Soviet citizen but was still within Soviet borders. Whoever it was among the top party officials that had authorized our release might fall from power—these changes occurred all the time. An overnight switch in policy toward the emigrants, a change in relations with the United States, or a mere remark made by an American congressman at which the Soviets took offense, could reverse our situation without warning. When the gate to freedom opened, we would make a run for it. We wouldn't stay one minute beyond the interval that would be required to pack our most essential belongings and fulfill all the legal and financial demands made by the government of people leaving the country.

I couldn't possibly sort out in my memory the details of those frantic days and nights. I had to cope with an unbelievable amount of red tape. I had often accompanied friends who were leaving Russia on their races through Moscow from bureau to department, from ministry to embassy, from bank to customs, where the emigrants had to fill out forms, obtain affi-

Forced to flee: Afghan girl

Forced to flee: Chinese sailor

davits, make any number of payments (both legal and bribes); seek officials' signatures, countersignatures, seals, and stamps; produce the enormous sheaf of documents a Soviet citizen has to accumulate—but not until my own permission came did I know what it was like to spend so many of my waking hours performing this staggering number of final duties.

I wonder if any slave ever felt as happy buying his own person from his owner as I felt in the savings bank, paying out 800 rubles for our exit visas: two small documents, printed on flimsy yellow paper. (The price for Jewish souls had gone way up since the start of the emigration: the authorities hadn't originally realized that not just a trickle, but tens of thousands of people would want to leave the country, and that a very profitable business could be made of this exodus.)

MARK YA AZBEL, refusenik, U.S.S.R

On July 24 they began to bombard, bombard, bombard. They shot bullets all over; it was a noise like one hears when it rains on the coffee trees. We heard the shots very well, and they fell like a light rain. We ran away in fright, in terror, because we had never heard so many shots before.

GUILLERMO MORALES PEREZ, *campesino,* Guatemala

I started my escape from Ben Tre in Western Saigon on May 22. There were 110 of us on a boat that was fifteen meters long, three meters wide. After three days, the transmission box broke, and some of us wanted to return. But others wanted to go on. The day after, the engine worked again, and when we passed Conson it stopped again. We floated the boat by wind and wave. On the ninth day, our food and water ran out. We were hungry and thirsty. Some started to weaken. We collected rain for drinking and tried to ration it. On the fourteenth day, a woman named Xuan was the first to die. We threw her body into the ocean. Some people tried to escape by making a wooden float. But all of them drowned or were missing when they tried to reach some passing ships. They were about twenty-four in all. On the nineteenth day, seven more died from weakness. We threw them overboard. On that same day at

"On the fourteenth day, a woman named Xuan was the first to die. We threw her body into the ocean. Some people tried to escape by making a wooden float. But all of them drowned."

8:30 AM two U.S. warships passed. One came within three-hundred meters of our boat. Four of us tried to swim to the vessel, but one drowned. There was an interpreter on the U.S. ship, who stood with a walky-talkie and told us, "Wait for the rescue by the other ships. They will come in two more days. We're on a dangerous mission. We'll give you food and water for survival." Two canoes brought us food—ham, water, apples, and oranges, One of the sailors photographed the floating body of the victim we threw into the ocean. Then they left.

We beat each other for the food. I took two boxes of meat, and I distributed it to the others. Afterwards, we felt better and bailed water out of the boat again. Six more days passed. Our food and water ran out. No ship rescued us. By June 28 we were very weak, and the water level in the boat was about one meter. We tried to bail but had no energy. One of us said, "We need food to survive." We talked together, and I asked the friend of Mr. Cuong, who was very weak, to kill Cuong for meat. His friends came closer to him and asked him. Then they told me what he said: "Please wait until tomorrow. I'll die. Then you'll eat me." We asked the passengers. They were silent. A group of us decided to kill Mr. Dao Hou Cuong. Three of us pulled Cuong out of the cabin and held his head in water. Then one of us butchered him. Four others helped. We cooked the meat in boiling water. One of the women cut the meat into small pieces and distributed it to the ones who bailed the water. Our group selected the good meat—liver and heart. We gave the others bones and bad meat. I remember we prayed to the Lord before we killed Mr. Cuong.

"See another body. Another, another. The body leaves a mark, so we know when the mines are there. Sometimes we don't know if the body is dead, or they fall asleep, or they still alive."

With the meat we were stronger and tried to bail water out. Again two days later a woman named Tram died from weakness. We butchered and cooked her also and ate her meat for two days. The next day, we caught a twelve-year-old boy named Nu, who was alive but very weak, and we drowned him (me and the group). Then we butchered him, boiled his meat, and ate again. By this time some passengers tried to jump into the sea to escape. But they were all drowned. Me and six others tried to make a float to escape, but after two kilometers we had to return. It was so very cold, and we were very weak.

The next day a child named Chau died. I didn't want to eat. A group butchered her. I tried to forget my hunger. But two days later, I couldn't. We nodded to a boy named Qui who was alive and not so weak. He understood, and he jumped into the cabin for protection from his cousin. I pulled him out, and we sank him in water. We needed twenty minutes to kill him. We butchered him and distributed the bad meat to the people who bailed out the water. A Philippine fishing boat rescued us one day later. All this I did to survive. I didn't want to kill, and I did not kill. I only kept the human meat. If I didn't, they would have all died. Some gave gold for meat, but I did not. I kept it for distributing to the passengers.

PHONG QUANG MINH, Vietnam

They say this is the border. But this isn't the end. Soldiers on the other side waiting to shoot you. We meet a trader. He tells us we have to walk along the border to find a camp, maybe another week. We have to pass O Chrau, it used to be a big trading place, and find the bridge into Thailand.

"What's that?" I ask the woman I go with. It's a bamboo stuck in the ground with a leaf on top of it.

She says it's good luck. But it smells bad here, funny, greasy, burning smell. Then I see it. The leg. Just a leg, lying there, black from sun, no person to go with it. Oh, no! Over there is a man without the leg.

"Mines."

The lady says it's a dangerous place. People go through here before us, they leave two or three bamboo sticks as a mark. This is a trail of the dead. See another body. Another, another. Their own body leaves a mark, so we know when the mines are there. Sometimes we don't know if the body is dead or they fall asleep or they still alive. Just keep running.

Mine blows up in front of us—*phhsssh-swok!* See a hand floating out of the air, it looks so natural, then a finger floats by. Natural as a leaf blowing in the wind.

Always scared now, all the time. My hands shake every minute. Big gun noise overhead—*blam! blam! blam!*—hear fighting all the time. Even when I sleep, I dream it's still happening. Imagine myself walking around a mine, imagine myself dropping down fast because a bomb just exploded. It's in your mind all the time. If I don't have all those things to think about, I don't know if I can go on.

You become accustomed to it. You even see people killed in front of your face, shot by the big gun or blown up; you see it all the time. Your eyes see, but your mind, it's not like a human mind anymore, it doesn't care what it sees.

I even see a head come off a body.

They tell us to run on top of the bodies. You can't step on a mine if you walk on the bodies that have already fallen. Can I do it? I just want to get over.

It funny. Doesn't bother me that much.

Pass O Chrau. See the river! Across the river, little Thailand house. Bridge is destroyed by the time we get there. Just put some tree across . . . have to go . . . keep going . . .

PHAT MOHM, ten-year-old girl, Cambodia

Forced to flee: Salvadoran mother

WHAT
BECOMES
HOME

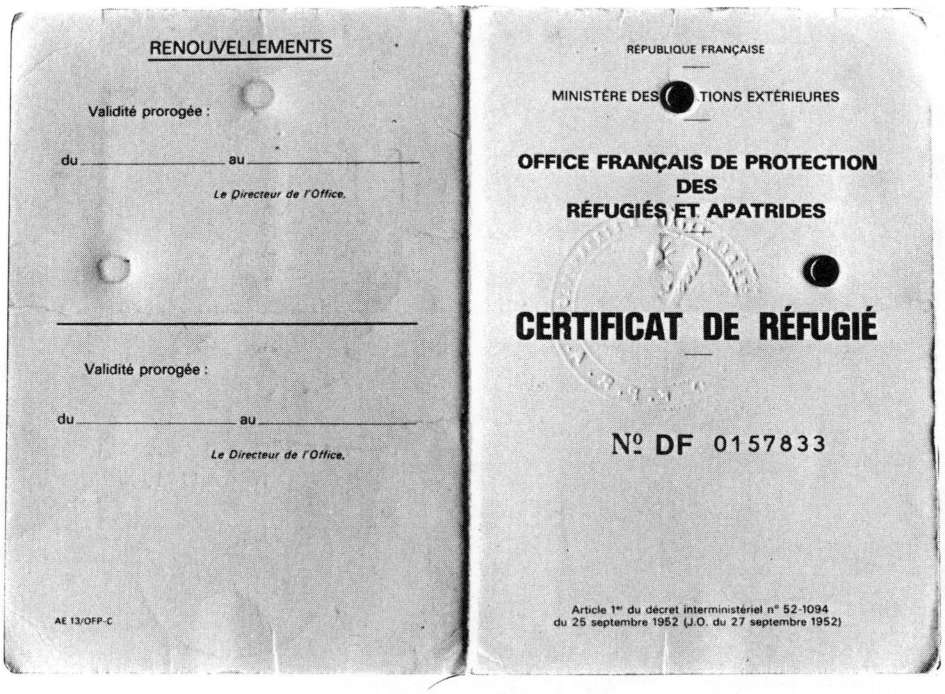

RENOUVELLEMENTS

Validité prorogée :

du _____ au _____

Le Directeur de l'Office.

Validité prorogée :

du _____ au _____

Le Directeur de l'Office.

AE 13/OFP-C

RÉPUBLIQUE FRANÇAISE

MINISTÈRE DES ⬤ TIONS EXTÉRIEURES

OFFICE FRANÇAIS DE PROTECTION
DES
RÉFUGIÉS ET APATRIDES

CERTIFICAT DE RÉFUGIÉ

№ DF 0157833

Article 1er du décret interministériel n° 52-1094
du 25 septembre 1952 (J.O. du 27 septembre 1952)

Refugee cards, like the one above issued in France, are provided by host governments and identify individuals who qualify for refugee status. The document is the refugee's "passport."

REFUGEE: Any person who, owing to well-founded fear of being persecuted for reason of race, religion, nationality, membership of a particular social group, or political opinion, is outside the country of his nationality and is unable or, owing to such fear, is unwilling to avail himself of the protection of that country; or who, not having a nationality and being outside the country of his former habitual residence, is unable or, owing to such fear, unwilling to return to it.

A newly arrived refugee is photographed with his documents at Phanat Nikhom transit center in Thailand. *Overleaf:* Mesa Grande camp, Honduras.

2.
HAVEN OR PRISON? INSIDE THE WORLD'S REFUGEE CAMPS

I'm so lucky I made it to this place. Amazing place. Nice and clean. You have a proper house. Everyone is sick like I am. I have a new feeling. This is where I belong.

The first day they give us crackers and milk. I never tasted milk. I hate it, but by then I'll eat anything. Then they give us a skirt, a blouse, shoes, a little round blue mirror. I don't want to look at my face. Somehow, I forgot how to use all those girly things.

They put all the children without parents together, in a center by ourselves, with wire all around. Like our own village. We have a long dormitory with a roof of woven palm leaf and bamboo beds raised up off the ground. They even give us a shelf over the bed to put your cup on.

This is a place I can't imagine. We have water, three tanks of it. Sometime I just sit to watch for the water truck, watch it fill up the tank with more water than we use up in a whole day. I can't remember much of how I got here. Everytime I open my mouth, the words I want scramble around. Can't say anything. I don't go out of the children's center for a pretty long time. I'm really scared of going out.

Sometimes at night I hear shooting. Shouts, screams. In the morning you see the people who got hurt, everything they have is stolen. Happens night after night. People say it's the Thai. Can't sleep without hearing screams.

My hair begins to fall out. I guess I'm sick in many ways. One day I'm alone in the dormitory. Sun flashes on the little blue mirror children hang over their beds; I decide to take a look at myself. That face, I can't ever forget it. It still gives me nightmares. For so long I never really looked at myself—in Pol Pot's time even I forgot if I'm a boy or a girl. Now I see a face, it doesn't even look human. It's an old face, dragged down under the eye, pale and yellow. The head is bare except for about fifty hairs, hanging like whiskers from an old man's chin.

PHAT MOHM, Cambodian, Khao I Dang camp, Thailand

Children stare through the barbed-wire fence surrounding Mesa Grande camp in Honduras. Housing 11,000 Salvadoran refugees up to October 1987 when some returned to El Salvador, many of them are survivors of the massacre at the Lempa River in 1981. Mesa Grande is in an isolated northwestern part of the country, some thirty-five kilometers from the Salvadoran border. It is the largest Honduran camp administered by the United Nations High Commissioner for Refugees.

Arriving in the area of settlement we were scared to death. You feel lost. You live in fear of starvation. You are shocked. Never had we seen such thick forest, inhabited only by wild animals, snakes, and big, biting flies. Homeland was a beautiful place, full of grazing cattle. My dreams are still bound to my homeland.

Ethiopian, locally settled in Somalia

This is a dentention camp and we are treated as prisoners. It seems that I just ran out of one prison to get into another. With 1,433 other refugees, I have been put in an ill-smelling windowless warehouse, used as a temporary detention ward. I need air more than anything else—air and space. I often cannot breathe. When suffocated by the sultry heat and lack of air, I usually wonder if I will get out of this camp alive. For a whole week, in spite of an awful backache, I had to sit day and night on the damp cemented floor, in the midst of heaps of luggage and people, before I could manage to get a little space to lie down at night, with my knees under my chin.

Vietnamese woman,
closed camp, Hong Kong

We are surrounded by Honduran troops here. At around six or seven at night, you start hearing shots up close, from the military outposts near here. And, although we'd like to go out on the hill, or take a walk in the street, it isn't possible. If I had known that I was going to be a prisoner in this camp beforehand, I never would have sought refuge.

NENA, Salvadoran,
Mesa Grande camp, Honduras

A typical "alley" in Mesa Grande camp, Honduras, consists of rows of wooden-frame shacks with corrugated tin roofs and walls of cardboard and burlap salvaged from discarded aid supplies. Refugees scour the barren terrain for valued firewood, used for cooking, shelter, and heat.

In June I was in Koya transit and I expected each to get a blanket, but to my surprise, we were given two blankets for eight people! At night I gave the blankets for the young children; I endured the coldness of the night. I didn't manage to bring my clothes, so right now I don't go to public places, because my rags do not allow me to do so.

Ugandan, Koya transit camp, Sudan

When we first came to Rafah in 1948, my father rented two rooms in the town for us all to live in. Then the United Nations began to build the camp in Rafah so we registered our name and were given a house. All the houses were the same—two rows in each block—each row, twenty houses. Ours had a roof like a fisherman's net; in the winter we used to catch the rain in our pans. We had paraffin lamps for lighting and heating and a standpipe in each row for water, which was switched on twice a day. My sister and I used to get up early to get a good place in the queue to be sure we got some water. After three years, we moved to another house in the camp. It was the same size as the first one, but there was some space at the back, so my father built two lean-tos as extra rooms. A United Nations Relief Works Agency (UNRWA) official came saying my father would have to pay a fine for encroaching on UNRWA land, but when he saw the conditions we were living in, he didn't have the heart to take any money off us.

AKRAM, Palestinian, Rafah camp, Gaza

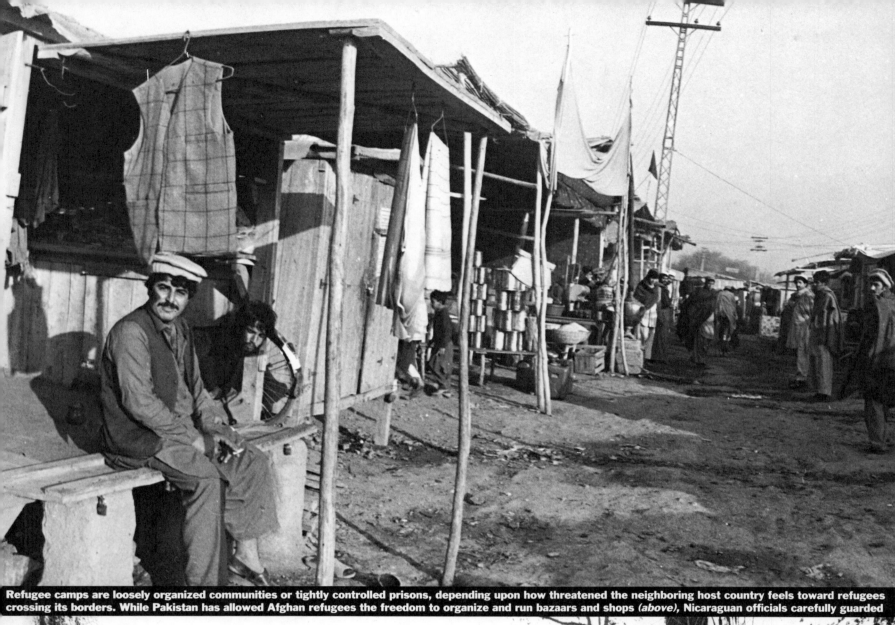

Refugee camps are loosely organized communities or tightly controlled prisons, depending upon how threatened the neighboring host country feels toward refugees crossing its borders. While Pakistan has allowed Afghan refugees the freedom to organize and run bazaars and shops *(above)*, Nicaraguan officials carefully guarded

the movements of Miskito Indians in Sahsa camp during 1982—84 *(below, left)*. Though conditions of poverty prevail in Scheiler camp, Jordan, the country offers refugees a semblance of normalcy by granting citizenship to the 870,000 Palestinians who live within its borders *(below, right)*.

We are mountain people and desert people, we are used to space—no one is cramped for space in Afghanistan, in the towns or out of them. The women had a good life before the Catastrophe; now they have all stopped singing; now they are cooped up like animals in their camps, with their children. Their men are fighting— they come and visit them between battles, sometimes with months between visits. The women are depressed and live on sedatives when they are lucky enough to get any. They cannot leave the camps—they are policed by the *mullahs* and by the Pakistani camp authorities. No, I am not criticizing the Pakistanis— without them we would all be dead; there would be no Afghans left.

Afghan in Pakistani camp

We are too many in a tent—no privacy. By the way, is the United Nations High Commission for Refugees (UNHCR) against refugees reproducing? A lot of us were killed; when can we replace them?

Ugandan in Sudan camp

After ten days in the camp we were permitted to go out to have a shower. We didn't have any bathroom. We showered under taps close to the ground. The men wore their shorts, and took a shower easily. But the women were deeply embarrassed. They had to wear their clothes to have a shower. I felt humiliated, but I had a great need to be clean! I hadn't washed for seventeen days since I had left Vietnam. I couldn't stand to be as dirty as I was. There were just about forty taps, but 3,000 people. So the refugees rushed and pushed at each other. Sometimes there were fights, and the fighters were sent to jail. There was a thirty-minute interval in which the people were allowed to shower. If you hadn't finished, or had just finished applying the soap to your body, that was your bad luck—no more water ran from the taps after that half hour.

WOO CHAN CHAN, Vietnamese, Kowloon
camp, Hong Kong

A Vietnamese refugee fills the tiny space she has claimed for herself in Canton camp, Hong Kong. Vastly overcrowded and understaffed, Hong Kong's eleven refugee camps house 25,000 refugees who have fled Vietnam. Many live in stacked compartments considerably less than the 3.5 square meters per person minimum emergency living space recommended by the World Health Organization.

What Becomes Home: *Left row, top to bottom:* One room housing ten Salvadorans, Mesa Grande camp, Honduras; sleeping shelf for Cambodians, Aranyaprathet camp, Thai-Cambodian border; flooded rooms in Hussein camp for Palestinians, Jordan; temporary quarters for East Europeans in Dortmund, Germany. *Right row, top to bottom:* A tent for newly arrived Nicaraguan refugees, Teupasenti camp, Honduras; Cambodian family, Mak Mun camp, Thai-Cambodian border; Greek Cypriot refugees, British Dhekelia Base, Cyprus; Afghan tent near Peshawar, Pakistan. *Opposite page:* tent interior for Mozambicans in Nyamatikiti camp, Zimbabwe.

We waited in lines for food. When it came, we could not swallow some of it. The rice was cooked in a way that scared us—very soft, filled with water and minced fish. It had a horrible smell. Even the children shook their heads.

TRAN THI NGA, Vietnamese in Guam camp

As you know, food is the most vital, fundamental factor of life. Without food we behave strangely. You can easily grow angry. You do not have any interest to converse with your friends. You think only of food. You can easily become a thief. You always look sick and gloomy. You always hate people talking to you. You can easily sell all your property and begin to beg from others. You always stay sick, fainting, and as well, die.

AKUTI SIMON, Ugandan in Sudan camp

Before we came here, we lived in the mountains. We were nomads. We have always been nomads, and we moved about freely. I have a wife and five children. We live here in the camp together with 30,000 other refugees. The life of our people in our homeland was like a dream. Now it is over.

I bought a lorry at home, and drove it across the border myself. Now every day I drive from the camp into the town and try to pick up a few good loads. If I'm lucky, I make a little money. In any case, it gives me a feeling of freedom.

Before, we lived off our flocks and the land. But today all my time is spent with the lorry. I've got a permit to drive in the border areas. It can be dangerous, but as nomads we have always moved freely across the border. We walked in the mountains, and it was cool and tranquil in the summer. Here it's hard to think. But God must give me a clear head and see to it that I get some work.

The chances are good at the bus stop, but it's a matter of being early. Nobody waits for you. There is nearly always somebody who wants something or other transported. But nobody's going to find the work for you. Everybody and his brother is doing it.

Young Tigrayans crowd around the water taps, turned on for a few hours a day, at Makalle camp for famine victims in northern Ethiopia. Since refugee camps are frequently built in remote, inaccessible areas, water sometimes has to be trucked in hundreds of miles. In dry seasons it is often rationed, and falls short of the fifteen liters recommended by the UNHCR for one person a day.

What to do now? Where to go and what to carry? OK, we pick up some vegetables and watermelons. I make a little money, but it goes mainly for petrol and repairs, and hiring people to help load the lorry. That leaves very little for me. Nevertheless, we get by.

It's too hot in the camp now. We aren't used to it, so I've driven most of the family up to the mountains, in the border country. They live up there the whole summer. I've got to stay here, in order to find something to haul. Now and then my eldest son and daughter visit me. So it isn't so lonely. In the meantime, we must try to live our lives here, and our brothers help us with shelter, food, and medical aid.
                    AFRIDAI, Afghan in Pakistani camp

Half of my family did not know where we were. I had everyone make signs with colored pencils. We all worked, putting them on tents, nailing them to trees.

The sign said, "Nga is in Tent 1005 at location such and such. Please get in touch." We heard nothing.

Once in a queue for food, I saw my nephew, who called, "Auntie, Auntie, I am out. My wife and children are stuck behind. I must fill the papers." Then he was swallowed by the door.

Many families were separated. Children wandered from tent to tent crying for their parents.
                    THAN TRI NGA, Vietnamese
                            in Guam camp

The years go by, and one day is just like another, and I have nearly stopped wondering what is going to happen with us. At one time we hoped to be able to return to our country, but it won't happen as long as there are foreign troops there. It's better to try to kill time than to be killed.

We have our daily life, and we live reasonably well. But it's crowded. There are many, many, many of us. The worst of it is not having anything to do. We're used to working the soil, and we've never been afraid of work. There are

A typical meal in Mesa Grande camp, Honduras, consists of nutritious beans, *tortillas*, and rice, served three times a day. Salvadorans in Mesa Grande cook their own meals with food supplied by the international community. Many refugees are forced to eat food cooked in communal kitchens or already prepared by camp officials. The UNHCR recommends a daily ration of over 2,000 calories a day for adults and children, but many refugees do not get enough to eat.

some good things in being here, of course. The women sew the way they always have, and the children go to school. We never did that. I have my smithy and my knives to make, and with a little luck I can sell one now and then.

Nobody here goes hungry, and we know that many people are helping us from outside, and we are very grateful. Still, it's strange being dependent on others, when you want to be managing for yourself and to support your family. And I've always been able to. That's something I often think about when I'm taking my walks. One must have something to think about.

SAINENG, Laotian,
Ban Vinai camp, Thailand

That day I got up, as usual, at 6 AM, and after breakfast my friends and I went singing along to the big tents in the camp's center that serve as our school. It was 7 AM and the bell had just signaled the start of classes. We were lining up when suddenly we heard a noise in the sky. There were planes dropping things and we said: "They are sending us more rations." A tragic mistake. These objects exploded as they touched the ground.

KOINI IDETE, Namibian,
Kassinga camp, South Angola

On January 16, I had permission to go into the town of Colomoncagua to buy some things. There were two of us, and as we were leaving a store, a captain and some soldiers captured us and took us to the command headquarters. There they beat us for being refugees, saying we were guerrillas. But we had permission to go into Colomoncagua to buy things, food, it was, that we needed at the camp. And so I said no, we weren't guerrillas, which was the truth.

That was at noontime. At 7 PM they put uniforms on us and took us out of the headquarters dressed like that, in uniform, so that the people in the town wouldn't recognize us, because they were going to kill us.

After we had walked for a while, they told my companion to lie down on the ground. His

A Tigrayan refugee at Fau camp, Sudan, angrily gestures that she has been given unmilled, unusable grain to eat *(near right)*. Another Tigrayan receives medicine at the International Red Cross clinic at Fau *(far right)*. For many refugees, the camp is their first exposure to health care, education and job training. International aid, intended to support a refugee in need, can upset cultural traditions and foster dependency by undermining the refugee's self-esteem, motivation, and self-reliance.

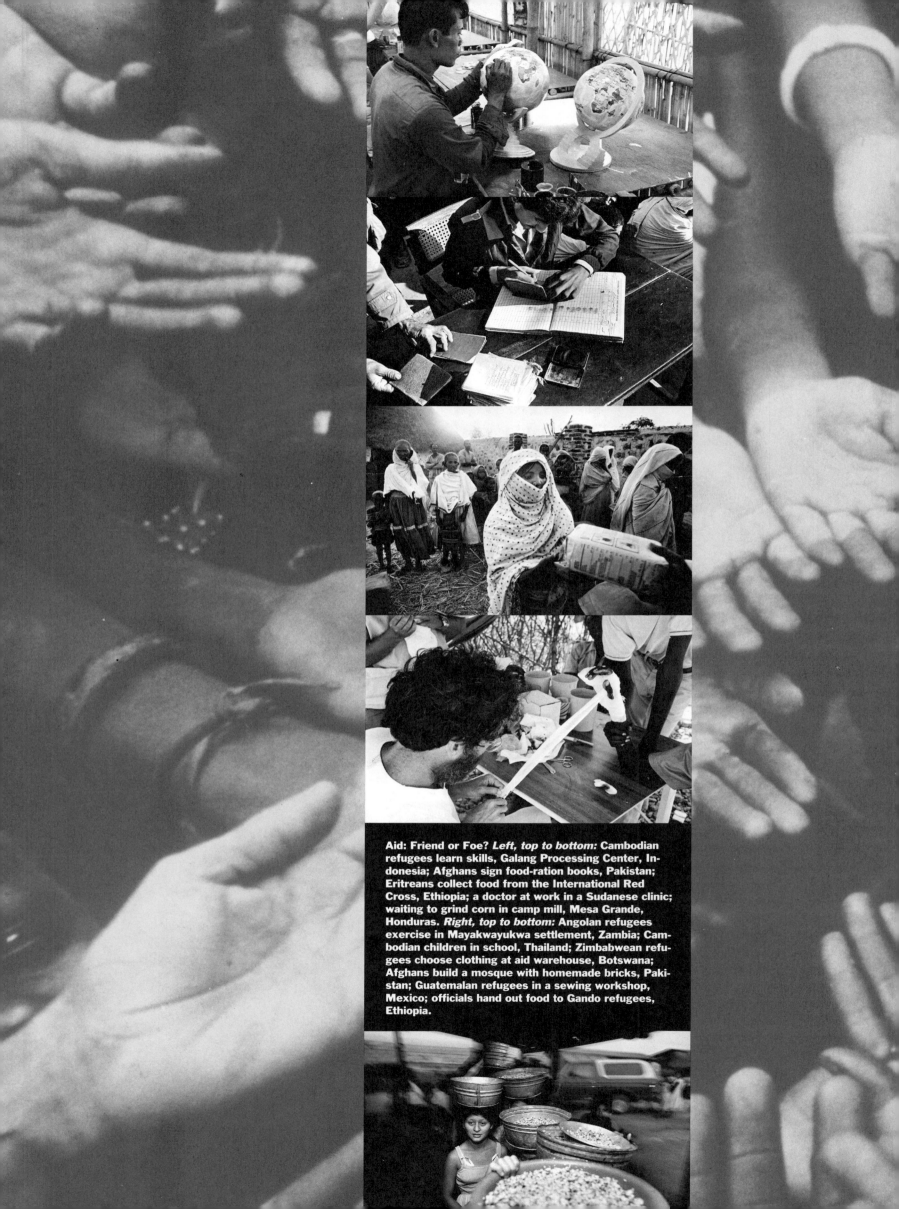

Aid: Friend or Foe? *Left, top to bottom:* Cambodian refugees learn skills, Galang Processing Center, Indonesia; Afghans sign food-ration books, Pakistan; Eritreans collect food from the International Red Cross, Ethiopia; a doctor at work in a Sudanese clinic; waiting to grind corn in camp mill, Mesa Grande, Honduras. *Right, top to bottom:* Angolan refugees exercise in Mayakwayukwa settlement, Zambia; Cambodian children in school, Thailand; Zimbabwean refugees choose clothing at aid warehouse, Botswana; Afghans build a mosque with homemade bricks, Pakistan; Guatemalan refugees in a sewing workshop, Mexico; officials hand out food to Gando refugees, Ethiopia.

name was Antonio Portillo, he was fifty-two years old, and he was a day laborer. They laid him out on the ground and tied his hands behind his back. They chopped at him three times with a machete and then shot a bullet into his head.

MIGUEL, Salvadoran,
Colomoncagua camp, Honduras

In the refugee camps (near the Sudan border) we were asked to go in one of the camp sites, far from the refugee office. Some friends told me it was dangerous. I met three other young refugees from Ankole, and we went together. When we reached the camp, people in camp asked to see our papers. Like my friends, I gave my education file, a written pass from the refugee office, and student card, etc. We asked to have them back, but they refused.

In the evening of the second night, I was

Refugees at Khao I Dang camp in Thailand (*left*) daily check the bulletin board, hoping to find news of missing relatives. Many refugees arriving in camps are missing family members, some through death, some through separation when they fled their homelands. An Ethiopian father in Somalia supports the head of his starving son (*below*), who died several days later. Malnutrition is the major cause of death in refugee camps, followed by measles, diarrheal diseases, malaria, and acute respiratory infections.

boiling dry beans when I saw a gang of people with ropes, knives, and sticks. I was with a boy called Jim in a tent, and other tentmates had gone to look for firewood. The gang surrounded us, and one old man among them started asking threatening questions: Who are we? Why we are here? Who gave us traveling permission? Which part of Uganda we came from? etc. He said everybody is watching us, and we could not go anywhere, even to the refugee office. I did not understand. One of them slapped my friend twice in the face. After three hours they left. A boy told us that if we can, we should leave the camp. He said we were risking death or torture. But my question was why?

That night I did not sleep. I heard everybody who was breathing and every noise of wind, insects, and birds. I was thinking; if I had a chance, I would get lost and never stay in the camps again.

JOHN KABITORO, Ugandan
in Sudan camp

It is a fact that our safety has not been guaranteed here, on the border; so how will it be guaranteed for us further into Honduras? There we will only go deeper into the pit, where there are more armed forces, and where they are going to repress us even more. We have become adjusted to the camps here. We have work here, work that was very hard for us to organize.

We have built everything here ourselves: the water tank, the health station, the houses, the latrines, the workshops. The old, the children, and the women are the ones who have built all this. Here, we have achieved a way of life where we share all our work, and we help each other very much. We live in a community and work collectively. We all take part in the decisions because we understand that our only hope for survival lies in sticking together.

FRANCISCO GOMEZ, Salvadoran,
Colomoncagua camp, Honduras

Since camps are often located close to borders, refugees are vulnerable to attack from the governments they are fleeing. They can also be harassed by the host country under whose control they fall. *Near right, top to bottom:* An Afghan settlement in Pakistan is reduced to rubble by a Soviet air-raid that killed some seventy people; Thai soldiers survey N/Gog camp, Kao Din, during a transfer of refugees to a site farther away from the Thai-Cambodian border; a Mozambican woman in Macovane refugee camp is wounded by an anti-personnel mine set by guerrillas to terrorize the camp's inhabitants. *Far right:* In Nicaragua, Salvadoran children practice a daily air-raid drill.

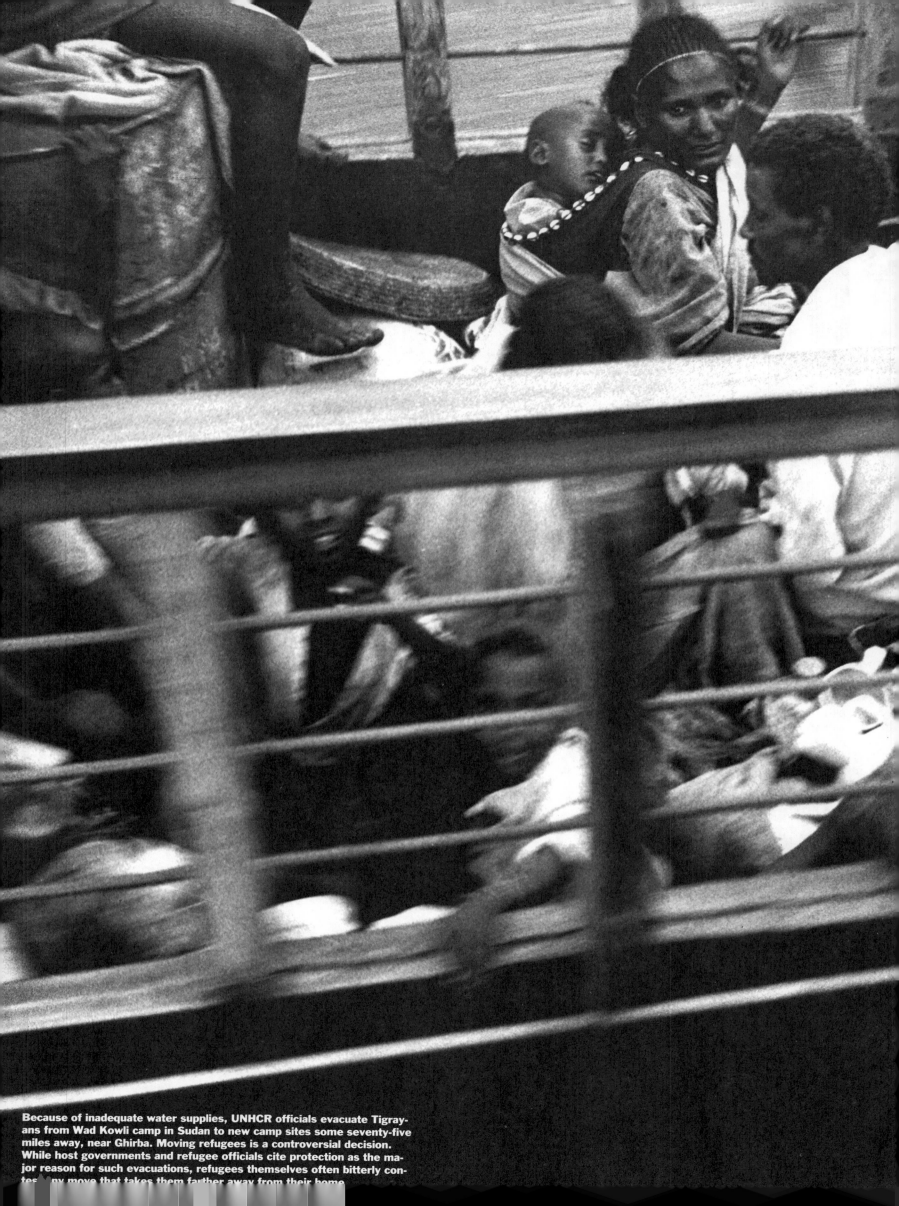

Because of inadequate water supplies, UNHCR officials evacuate Tigrayans from Wad Kowli camp in Sudan to new camp sites some seventy-five
miles away, near Ghirba. Moving refugees is a controversial decision.
While host governments and refugee officials cite protection as the major reason for such evacuations, refugees themselves often bitterly con-
test any move that takes them farther away from their home.

SOME FACTS YOU SHOULD KNOW: LIFE IN THE WORLD'S REFUGEE CAMPS

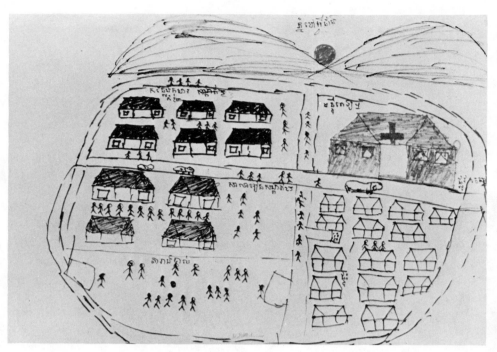

Child's drawing of Khao I Dang refugee camp, Thailand.

First UNHCR aid to refugee outflow: Berlin crisis, 1953

Refugees in camps as of January 1, 1987: 5,600,488

Percentage of refugees from third world: over 90

Percentage who seek asylum in third world: 95

Average per capita for nations of first asylum: $822

Percentage of refugees who are Afghan: 43

Percentage who are in Africa: 28

Percentage who are women and children: over 75

Average length of stay in camp: 5 plus years

Longest stay: 40 years (Palestinians)

Date of first closed camp where refugees are confined and not allowed to seek outside work: 1940, Switzerland, internment camp for Jews

Recommended emergency living space per person according to World Health Organization: 3.5 square meters

Refugee children of primary school age: 2.5 million

Children receiving primary education in UNHCR programs: 320,000

Leading causes of death, mostly preventable, in camps: malnutrition, measles, diarrheal diseases, malaria, and acute respiratory infections

1987 UNHCR budget for general programs: $348,900,000

Percentage of 1970 UNHCR funds devoted to long-term solutions: 80

Percentage of 1986 funds: 40

Percentage of refugees who repatriated in 1987: 1.5

Percentage who achieved self-sufficiency in country of first asylum in 1987: 12

Percentage who resettled in third country: 1

ETHIOPIANS IN SUDAN AND SOMALIA

Total population: 1.1 million

Life expectancy: 40 years

Ratio of Ethiopian refugees to African refugee population: 1 to 4

Number killed by famine 1984—85: 1 million

Number dependent on emergency food assistance 1988: 5—7 million

Refugees in Sudan: 677,000

Number of UNHCR rural settlements, where refugees have land and are reasonably self-sufficient: 21

Number settled in countryside with assistance from UNHCR: 246,000

Refugees in Somalia: 430,000

Number according to Somalian government: 840,000

Number of UNHCR camps: 43

Percentage of UNHCR budget directed to Somalia: 8

CAMBODIANS IN THAILAND

Total population: 314,579

Number of UNHCR-registered refugees, most of whom have been rejected for resettlement: 14,579

Unregistered, unassisted, unprotected refugees, classified as "displaced persons," living along Thai-Cambodian border: 300,000

Fourth biggest "city" in Thailand: Site 2 camp, population 165,000

Camps supervised by UNHCR: 1

Camps supervised by UNBRO (United Nations Border and Relief Organization): 8

Miles covered by border camps: 400

Percentage of population in border camps under four years of age: 25

Percentage over sixteen years with no means of employment: 51

Cost of maintaining U.N. border relief program in 1987: $36 million

VIETNAMESE IN HONG KONG

Total population: 25,000

Number of open camps: 1

Closed camps: 5

Detention centers: 5

Refugees in open camps (those who arrived before July 2, 1982): 2,600

In closed camps: 13,500

In detention centers: 9,300

Number who arrived by boat in 1987: 3,026

Number who arrived by boat through June 1988: over 7,700

Percentage who have been in camps four or more years: almost 50

Cost to Hong Kong of maintaining refugees from 1979 to December 1987: $101.8 million

Refugees resettled in third country in 1980: 37,468

In 1987: 2,212

Country receiving greatest number of Hong Kong refugees for resettlement from 1975–87: United States

Percentage drop in resettlement to United States from 1986 to 1987: 75

PALESTINIANS IN JORDAN, LEBANON, GAZA STRIP, WEST BANK, AND SYRIA

Total population: 2.3 million

Number living in camps: 793,000

Number of camps: 61

Areas in which refugees have rights of citizenship: Jordan and West Bank

Average age of refugees: 27 years

Annual budget of United Nations Relief and Works Agency (UNRWA): $216 million

Percentage allocated to education: 70

Health care: 20

Relief: 10

Amount of Israeli aid to occupied territories in 1987: $240 million

Amount collected by Israeli government in taxes: $393 million

Refugee children receiving education at UNRWA schools in 1988: 349,000

Patient/visits to UNRWA health services per year: 6.2 million

Population density in Gaza Strip: 4,500 people per square mile

Per capita income 1988: $1,000

Number who work in Israel: 45–65,000

Percentage of population in Gaza who are refugees: 80

Percentage of population in West Bank who are refugees: 38

Per capita income in 1988: $1,400

Average yearly number of violent demonstrations since 1982 by Palestinians under Israeli occupation (before the *intifadeh*): 3,000

AFGHANS IN PAKISTAN

Total population: 3.5 million

Ratio of refugees to Pakistanis: 1 to 33

Number of refugee camps: 328

Maximum recommended number of refugees permitted by Pakistan per camp: 10,000

Largest number registered in a camp: 30,000

Percentage of people over forty-five years of age: less than 10

Percentage under fifteen years: 57

Percentage born in camps: 24

Number of livestock accompanying refugees: 3 million

Daily ration each refugee receives: 500 grams flour, 20 grams sugar, 1.5 grams tea, 30 grams cooking oil, 30 grams dry skimmed milk

Percentage of cost of refugee care borne by Pakistan: 50

Hospital beds in Peshawar for refugees: 1,300

Number reserved for women: 110

Ratio of doctors to refugees: 1 to 15,000

Artificial limbs provided to refugees through 1986: 10,061

Refugees killed in camps and villages along border by Soviet and Afghan air raids and artillery barrages: 4,000

Estimated cost of helping Afghans return home, including six months of food rations: over $1.5 billion

Estimated cost per refugee: $35–$200

Percentage of returning refugees international community can assist during first year: 20

MOZAMBICANS IN MALAWI, SOUTH AFRICA, ZIMBABWE, ZAMBIA, SWAZILAND, AND TANZANIA

Total population: 1,193,250

People internally displaced: over 2 million

Number of camps: 10

Miles covered by electrified fence erected by South Africa along Mozambique border: 43

Estimated number of refugees entering South Africa monthly during 1987: 1,200

Estimated number of refugees forcibly returned to Mozambique monthly in 1987: 2,000

Percentage of refugees registered with South African authorities: 20

Number of refugees working illegally in South Africa: 180,000

Number in Zimbabwe who are self-settled: 30,000

Number expelled from Zimbabwe to Mozambique in 1987: 15,000

Number arriving daily in Malawi in 1988: 1,000

Percentage who voluntarily repatriated in 1987: less than 1

Percentage who were resettled in third country in 1987: 0

THE REFUGEE CAMP: SOLUTION OR PROBLEM?

MARK MALLOCH BROWN

At the time of writing, there is a slim chance the world's largest refugee camps may be closed down. The Afghans may—and it is a big may—be about to go home in the wake of the Geneva peace agreement. If all goes according to plan, the number of refugees in camps around the world will be halved at a stroke. With the exodus of the Afghans from Pakistan, refugee camps will have fulfilled the purpose they were meant for: to provide a temporary sanctuary until people can go home. Unfortunately, camps rarely function that way. More typical is a shallow ex-paddy field that lies at the foot of a low-slung hill some five miles or so into the Thai side of the Thai-Cambodian border. The hill is called Khao I Dang, and it gave its name to a refugee camp which became, for a few brief months in 1979 and 1980, the most famous in the world. In the pre-Christmas season of 1979, with President Carter and Senator Edward Kennedy fighting for the conscience of their party's activists, the Cambodians briefly caught the compassion of America and the world. Mrs. Carter even visited. Then international attention passed on to other human dramas and political upheavals—1980 was the year Iran held the American hostages in Tehran, the Afghans began to flee into Pakistan. Khao I Dang was forgotten.

Created during a flash storm of international concern, Khao I Dang was left to fend for itself when public opinion shifted to other news events. Nine years later, the office of the United Nations High Commissioner for Refugees still assists its inhabitants and seeks to resettle them, with less and less success, in North America, Europe, and Australia. The Thai government, exasperated by the failure to find any permanent solution for the remaining 14,579 refugees, has officially closed the camp. But Khao I Dang remains, stubbornly refusing to go away, as the refugees despair of salvation from their precarious plight.

The Thai government's action is unusual. Most host countries prefer to advertise their refugee camps as a way of drumming up foreign assistance. Indeed, what characterizes the modern camp is how political interests converge to maintain it. Governments see the camp as the most convenient way to corral unwanted visitors; together with international relief agencies, they come to view it as an unequaled fund-raising tool. The camp focuses donors' attention and is tangible proof of a need. Even the refugees' own political leaders recognize the advantages of camp life as a way of keeping their cause before the world. The Afghans, the Palestinians, the refugees of Central America, and the refugees of the Horn of Africa have all maintained political solidarity in exile through the tight leadership structures possible in the confined space of a camp.

We have grown so used to the image of the refugee in a camp, helplessly staring out at us through barbed wire, that we often do not think of asking the important question: Are camps a good way of caring for refugees?

Camps are supposed to be a temporary solution. They functioned this way during the last forty years in the Indian subcontinent, where massive flows of Pakistanis, Burmese, and Bangladeshis were held in camps until a solution was brokered to allow their return home. These people have been the exception rather than the rule. Ask the refugees who have been stranded in "temporary" camps for years, or even generations. Camps have often prolonged, not solved, refugee problems, because when no grand political solution is available, refugees find all other options are gone. They cannot slip home on their own or melt into the local population.

It is commonly believed that by concentrating refugees in one place it is easier to bring them the food, shelter, clean water, sanitation, and the health care on which their survival depends. Concentrating them in one place, however, also increases their health risk and makes them dependent on international relief. Left to their own devices to live off the land and borrow from sympathetic locals, refugees usually do much better than their anxious overseers from the international aid agencies recognize. In southern Sudan in the early 1980s, refugees from Uganda, as in many other parts of Africa, had been living among the Sudanese without any discernibly greater problems than the local population. Then a second wave of Ugandans required camps because of renewed fighting in Uganda, and before long the older group of refugees, drawn to them for the protection, food, and medical care they offered, ended up in the new settlements too.

Like Cambodians, Nicaraguans, Afghans, and almost any other refugee population that suddenly finds itself living on top of its neighbors, the Ugandans began to succumb to public health problems that they had never before been exposed to. Drinking water was quickly polluted, and open defecation, never a problem for dispersed rural communities, was suddenly a threat to their own and their neighbors' health. At the same time, they found themselves totally dependent on outsiders for food. They had no access to fields or shops.

Humanitarian aid organizations take the position that refugees are best protected in a camp setting. Certainly, in the first chaotic weeks of a refugee influx it is hard to monitor peoples' safety if they are dispersed. Every arrival of vulnerable, unarmed people—mostly women and children—seems to provoke cruel atrocities. Nevertheless, over the long term camps do become targets of abuse. The international officials, who busy themselves assembling the refugees in one place so they can better protect them, soon find they are not policemen. Quoting international legal statutes about refugee rights is scant protection against rape, theft, extortion, military recruitment, and attack. Who can doubt that camps have, over time, added to the vulnerability of Palestinians and Cambodians? Sanctuary too quickly turns to target.

14 MILLION REFUGEES: WHO ARE THEY? WHERE ARE THEY?

WHO THEY ARE	WHERE THEY GO (Countries of First Asylum)	
Afghanistan: 5,751,000	Pakistan	3,541,400
	Iran	2,200,000
	India	5,600
	Kuwait	4,000
Palestinians: 2,268,000*	Jordan	870,000
	Gaza Strip	459,000
	West Bank	386,000
	Lebanon	288,000
	Syria	265,000
Mozambique: 1,193,250	Malawi	610,000
	South Africa	250,000
	Zimbabwe	166,250
	Tanzania	72,000
	Swaziland	60,000†
	Zambia	35,000
Ethiopia: 1,122,300	Sudan	677,000
	Somalia	430,000†
	Djibouti	13,500
	Kenya	1,800
Iraq: 470,000	Iran	410,000
	Turkey	60,000
Angola: 404,000	Zaire	310,000
	Zambia	94,000
Somalia: 400,000	Ethiopia	400,000
Cambodia: 335,800	Thailand	314,570
	Vietnam	21,000
	Philippines (Refugee Processing Center)	230
Sudan: 301,000	Ethiopia	300,000
	Uganda	1,000
Burundi: 244,000	Tanzania	160,000
	Rwanda	74,000
	Zaire	10,000
Rwanda: 196,700	Uganda	118,000
	Burundi	65,800
	Zaire	11,000
	Kenya	1,900
Western Sahara: 165,000	Algeria	165,000†
El Salvador: 152,000**	Mexico	120,000†
	Honduras	13,300
	Nicaragua	7,800
	Costa Rica	6,200
	Belize	3,800
	Panama	800
	Guatemala	100
China (Tibet): 100,000	India	100,000
Philippines: 90,000	Malaysia	90,000
Sri Lanka: 85,000	India	85,000
Iran: 80,100***	Iraq	75,000
	Pakistan	4,000
	India	1,100
Laos: 78,500	Thailand	75,580
	Philippines	2,920

WHO THEY ARE	WHERE THEY GO (Countries of First Asylum)	
Namibia: 77,860	Angola	70,000
	Zambia	7,500
	Sierra Leone	160
	Cameroon	100
	Nigeria	100
Vietnam: 68,520	Thailand	15,710
	Hong Kong	25,000
	Philippines	3,890
	Philippines (Refugee Processing Center)	4,910
	Malaysia	15,000
	Indonesia	2,490
	Japan	590
	Macau	550
	Singapore	200
	China	100†
	Korea	80
Chad: 63,500	Sudan	45,000
	Cameroon	5,000
	Central African Republic	5,000
	Nigeria	4,000
	Benin	3,700
	Congo	700
	Ghana	100
Yemen (People's Democratic Republic): 61,200	Yemen Arab Republic	61,200
Nicaragua: 55,300**	Honduras	32,000
	Costa Rica	23,000
	Guatemala	300
Zaire: 54,900	Tanzania	16,000
	Angola	13,000
	Burundi	9,600
	Zambia	9,500
	Sudan	5,000
	Uganda	1,400
	Congo	400
Bangladesh: 50,000	India	50,000
Guatemala: 46,520**	Mexico	45,000
	Belize	500
	Honduras	500
	Nicaragua	400
	Bolivia	120
South Africa: 28,800	Angola	9,000
	Swaziland	7,000
	Tanzania	6,000
	Zambia	3,000
	Lesotho	2,000†
	Botswana	700
	Zimbabwe	500
	Nigeria	400
	Mozambique	200
Burma: 20,000	Thailand	20,000
Uganda: 16,900	Sudan	10,000
	Kenya	4,500
	Zaire	2,000
	Burundi	400
Romania: 10,000	Hungary	10,000

WHO THEY ARE	WHERE THEY GO (Countries of First Asylum)	
Suriname: 8,000	French Guiana	8,000
Haiti: 8,000**	Dominican Republic	6,000
	Cuba	2,000
Chile: 6,080	Argentina	5,500
	Ecuador	480
	Bolivia	100
Guinea-Bissau: 5,400	Senegal	5,400
Zimbabwe: 4,000	Botswana	4,000
Cuba: 2,500	Costa Rica	2,500
Ghana: 1,300	Togo	1,200
	Ivory Coast	100

*Palestinians: There are an estimated 4 million Palestinians worldwide, 2,268,000 of whom have been registered by UNWRA as refugees.
**El Salvador, Nicaragua, Guatemala, and Haiti: Hundreds of thousands of undocumented Central Americans in refugee-like circumstances reside in the United States and other countries.
***Iran: About one million Iranians live in exile, only a small percentage of whom have been officially recognized as refugees.
†Sources vary widely

Source: U.S. Committee for Refugees, Washington, D.C., as of November 1988.

The pediatric ward for Ethiopian refugees at Korem, Ethiopia.

Refugees who require international protection and/or assistance may be new populations or may have been in a country for years. They are unable to repatriate because of a continued fear of persecution in their homelands and are unable to find permanent settlement in their country of asylum or elsewhere. Not included are the millions of undocumented aliens and asylum seekers living in the United States, Europe, and the Middle East, many of whom deserve refugee status.

DEC.15,1984 -CRDA CONFIRMS ICA.
TO WORK WITH ICA.
-25 TONS OF PROTEIN BLEND
DEC.19,1984 FOOD SHIPPED TO ADDIS ABBA
(CRDA) FOR ICA FIELD TEAM
(DUE TO ARRIVE JAN.10-12). $12,500
DEC.21,1984 -LANDCRUISER SHIPPED TO
ADDIS ABBA FOR ICA TEAM
(DUE TO ARRIVE JAN.10). $10,000
-MEDICAL SUPPLIES FOR
(MSF) VIA ETHIOPIAN AIRLINES. $115,075
DEC.31,1984 -FUNDS REMITTED FOR
ETHIOPIAN FIELD OPERATIONS.

WHO'S PAYING THE BILL?
TOP TWENTY DONORS 1987

United States	$226.3 million
European Economic Community	86.1 million
Japan	75.2 million
Germany	55.2 million
United Kingdom	36.3 million
Sweden	31.8 million
Canada	31.4 million
Denmark	30.3 million
Switzerland	24.7 million
Norway	24.6 million
Italy	24.2 million
Netherlands	19.5 million
Finland	8.3 million
Australia	5.5 million
Belgium	4.4 million
France	4.0 million
Spain	2.1 million
Saudi Arabia	1.6 million
Kuwait	1.2 million
Israel	.9 million

Joe Bass, founder of International Christian Aid, explains to the press how donations were allotted for famine victims in Ethiopia.

A barge loaded with rice seed donated by Oxfam, an English relief organization, lands in Phom Penh port, Cambodia *(above)*. Workers *(left)* in a therapeutic feeding center at Fau camp, Sudan.

TOP DONORS
According to
Contribution Per Capita

Denmark	$5.94
Norway	5.86
Sweden	3.79
Switzerland	3.74
Finland	1.69
Netherlands	1.34
Canada	1.21
United States	.93
Germany (FRG)	.90
Luxemburg	.82
United Kingdom	.64
Japan	.62
Kuwait	.61
Belgium	.45
Italy	.42
Australia	.34
Ireland	.21
Iceland	.21
Israel	.20

Amounts based on estimated 1987 contributions to UNHCR, Intergovernmental Committee for Migration, and UNRWA

Emergency relief is trucked into Tigray, Ethiopia, *(far left)*. Two major providers of aid are the United States, which donated 64,000 tons of vegetable oil to African countries in 1988, and the E.E.C., suppliers of 20,000 tons of cereals in 1988 to Sudan *(above)*.

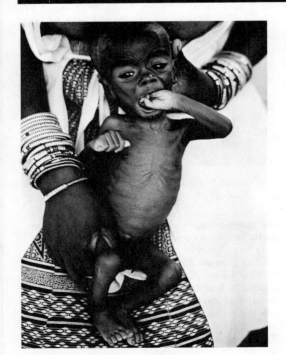

Starving South African baby

WHEN AID STOPS: HOW THE BODY STARVES

It is incomprehensible for one who has never experienced starvation to understand the physical cycle of the symptoms of starvation. The first few days the stomach complains with cramps and bloating while it gradually shrinks in size. Water helps a little and is used as a primary supplement for those dietary faddists who want to take off thirty pounds a month. Deficiency diseases are prevented in this group by the addition of adequate vitamin supplements. Often tranquilizers, and other medications are used to suppress appetite and allay the cramping pains of an angry, protesting stomach. Unfortunately, however, when you don't have vitamins and these other supplemental niceties, the game is for keeps. Starving children cry the first few days and eat anything to stop hunger pains. Rags, straw, clay, chalk, and even poisonous weeds, berries, and twigs have been reportedly ingested. As weakness increases, cries change to whimpers. Then there is the nausea. This comes while nature is burning all of the body's fat from the muscles and all the other tissues where it is deposited. The burning of the fat without adequate carbohydrates (sugar and starch) produce acidosis. The fruity odor of acetone can be detected on the breath, and acetone also appears in the urine. This same condition occurs in diabetics on improperly balanced diets, and if not corrected goes on to severe acidosis, diabetic coma, and death. Nature becomes kinder to the starving at this juncture, kinder than the politicians arguing about boundaries and power. A great overpowering lethargy develops, and a kind and wise nature offers large doses of sleep to ease the pain of slow death. In the meantime the body proteins have been depleted, the water and electrolyte balance destroyed. The abdomen becomes distended with fluid, the extremities swollen with water, and now the degeneration of the vital organs such as the liver and the kidneys starts in earnest. At this stage the individual's ability to combat other diseases gradually decreases, and he may be mercifully spared further suffering by the terminal effects of any type of infection. At this juncture, if nutrition is restored and the patient recovers, it is often with permanent damage to the vital organs either from the ravages of starvation or the after-effects of infection. These complications may lead to chronic invalidism and premature death. What a price for innocent people to pay for power politics. HOWARD A. RUSK, M.D.

While North America and Europe may be able economically to support extra mouths, developing economies cannot. The predictable government response is to segregate the refugees in camps and ration out food provided by the international community—the ultimate soup kitchen. Yet this response ignores the repeated economic impact of refugees, which is as an engine of growth, not burden, on their host societies. Nobody can doubt that the East African Asians, who fled Idi Amin's Uganda, have been a dynamic force in Britain and a corresponding loss for Uganda. Similarly, the Vietnamese have quickly become mainstays of the small retail sector in the United States and in France.

The Afghans in Pakistan, who benefit from the biggest internationally funded camp program in the world, are fortunately too numerous and powerful to be deterred by an alliance of international pampering and local Pakistani control. The presence of two and one-half million Afghans has led to a significant increase in, among other things, Pakistani transport services, which the Afghans now in considerable part control. Far from draining Pakistan, the return of the refugees to Afghanistan will leave a hole in the Pakistani economy. In the end, Pakistan has benefited three ways: 1) Afghan enterprise has spurred the Pakistani economy; 2) international assistance to the Afghans has also provided improved services for Pakistan; and 3) the war between the Soviets and Afghanistan has allowed Pakistan to be a major supplier to the rebel effort.

Refugee camps, barring those in the Middle East, are off the front page. The most controversial new refugee flows have been directly into Western Europe and the United States—Iranians and Tamils into Europe and Central Americans into the United States. Yet there is no reason to suppose the media's lack of interest will continue. As soon as the next third world upheaval occurs, there is little doubt governments and aid agencies will again make news when they reach out for their ready-made solution—the refugee camp. In doing so they may again contribute to an extension of, not a solution to, the refugee problem.

But there is a way out of this tired response to refugee outflows. As with most fresh thinking in the refugee industry, it starts with the refugees themselves. When in 1984 Tigrayans, victims of famine and war, made their way out of Ethiopia into eastern Sudan, their leaders were wary of the welfare net of camps. They were afraid camp dependency would quickly set in, and when the famine eased, the Tigrayans, settled into a false comfort, would not want to go home. Their solution was to take the food aid but close the camps to the foreign relief workers poised to install and administer relief programs. By making sure the camp arrangements were temporary, nobody had a chance to settle down. In the end, there was no institutionalizing of the Tigrayans.

Another less happy example concerns Nicaraguan Miskito Indians who sought refuge in the Honduran side of Mosquitia in 1982. More urbanized than their Honduran neighbors, the Miskitos nonetheless felt a greater affinity with their fellow Indians in Honduras than with the government in Managua, whatever its political complexion. The pace of exodus picked up when the conflict grew from one of meddling modernizers in Managua seeking to impose various central government policies on the Miskitos, to a regional struggle in the spotlight of world attention.

As a group, the Miskitos combine a wariness of outsiders with an astonishing facility for suddenly throwing themselves on the mercy of international relief workers. This contradictory behavior appears to come from their history of contacts with waves of European missionaries arriving on the Atlantic Coast bearing gifts as well as bibles. After a hurricane in the 1960s, the Miskitos virtually gave up work for several years until the international disaster relief ran out. With their susceptibility to welfare handouts, the Miskitos were obvious candidates for camps when they fled Nicaragua. Yet those involved in setting up the camp program were reluctant to take this approach precisely because of the dependency it would spawn.

The onset of the rainy season and the inaccessibility of Honduran Mosquitia, where the refugees were gathered, forced the creation of a temporary camp, Mocoron. However, against the refugees preference, plans were put in motion to disperse them to designated rural settlement areas when the planting season arrived. The intention was to take advantage of both the availability of land in underpopulated Honduran Mosquitia and the ethnic ties between locals and refugees. Seeds and tools were provided and a schedule announced for phasing out food aid. The program got off to an excellent start. It was undone by well- intentioned but disastrous congressional action in Washington. Anxious to block military aid to the Nicaraguan *contras,* Congress insisted the money be put to humanitarian use instead. This policy decision inadvertently bolstered the agendas of the administration, the *contras,* and the Honduran government, each of which had its reasons for wanting the Miskitos to remain dependent. The administration needed a captive population to fight alongside the *contras,* the *contras* desperately needed able guerrilla fighters, and the Honduran government needed assurances that the refugees, deprived of their old livelihoods, would not settle permanently within Honduras. The net result of United States government action was that rations and other temporary relief were reinstated, and the Miskitos were soon enjoying congressional beneficence.

Refugees' best hopes lie in becoming self-sufficient. International donors have no monopoly on charity. Local communities are usually all too willing to share their meager resources with the refugee. Aid agencies should not strive to remove the refugee from this community to the apartheid of a camp, except as an absolute last resort. Rather, their goal should be to help the refugee become an asset to his new community. This can be accomplished, in the first place, by directing development funds to local communities to increase their infrastructure and employment possibilities in order to meet the new demands created by a refugee influx; and secondly, by determining what the refugee needs to achieve his full economic and social potential in his new setting.

The energy the Cambodians at Khao I Dang expended in the early years in seeking to re-create their old way of life would have been much better spent establishing real communities than on maintaining the bamboo Disneyland that Khao I Dang became. A refugee problem is never solved by letting refugees pile up in camps, a human flotsam left behind when the tide of public interest recedes. Refugees must be made a living and dynamic part of the communities where they seek refuge. In this, not in international handouts, lies the prospect of a reasonable life in exile.

PAINFUL CHOICES: TERRIBLE ODDS

A *campesina* rebuilds her destroyed home in the highlands of Guatemala. In 1987 significant voluntary repatriations occurred in Uganda, Chad, Ethiopia, El Salvador, Nicaragua, and Haiti. Worldwide only one-and-a-half percent of the refugees who must flee their countries are able to return home.

GOING HOME: THE FIRST CHOICE

Refugee camps in the Municipality of Trinitaria,
Chiapas, Mexico. November 8, 1986
President of the Republic of Guatemala,
Marco Venicio [sic] Cerezo A.
National Palace
His office

Mr. President,

On behalf of all the refugee camps located in Chiapas we send you the cordial greetings you deserve. We hope you are in very good health along with the other state authorities.

After this brief greeting we move on to the following points:

First:

We learned about our repatriation from the radio and that conversations are being held with the Mexican government of Miguel de la Madrid Hurtado and other international organizations such as the United Nations High Commisssion for Refugees, consuls, and ambassadors. Also, that the Guatemalan government is concerned about the 40,000 refugees located in the Mexican States of Chiapas, Campeche, and Quintana Roo.

Second:

The situation in which we refugees live and have lived has been cruel because we have suffered in all kinds of ways, and we know that all the previous governments have continually deceived us with their policies. They offered us many things, but in the end they only gave us death. That's why we worry about returning to your country. We fear the same thing will happen to us. Now then, as head of the present government you offer us democracy and liberty and say that massacres and violence no longer exist in our country. We would like that very much if it were true and the life of all human beings was respected. We ask you, as you have been concerned about us, to fulfill the following conditions:

a) We are very much in agreement in recognizing our country where we were born, because we are anxious to go and work on our land and not be refugees, without land like we are now. We do not agree to go and live in the development poles that are being prepared for us. We are agreed that the land we came from should be recognized as ours.

b) Indemnity must be granted for the belongings we lost, such as our coffee fields, cardamom, houses, animals, fruit trees, etc., destroyed by the Army.

c) Nor do we want to go on patrol in the paramilitary bands. We ask for the complete dissolution of the civil self-defense patrols because they are not in our interests. That is what the Army is for, to give security, not an unarmed civilian whom they push straight into the line of fire. This has caused the death of many innocent and defenseless peasants. We don't want to be slaves while they talk to us of democracy and liberty, saying that they are carrying out the laws of the constitution of the republic.

d) We ask you as the present government concerned for our return, to take responsibility for the safety of our lives upon our return. We don't want to be kidnapped or murdered by the Army.

e) Mr. President: if you are really a democratic government, we ask you as the highest authority to bring to justice the high-ranking military men such as Romeo Lucas García, Efraín Ríos Montt, and Oscar Mejía Víctores. They governed cruelly and massacred our loved ones. But the blood shed cries out for the perpetrators to be brought to justice. We know very well that here in this world there will be justice and peace and love for one's neighbors as the Holy Scriptures say.

f) We ask you to carry out the agrarian reform because that is what interests us as peasants. We are drawn towards the earth because we live off the land and it sustains us with all its produce. We are the producers of corn, beans, wheat, rice, coffee, cardamom, etc. The land is of vital importance to us.

Mr. President: I hope that our above mentioned requests will be taken into account so that we will return with every joy, because should it be otherwise, we would be unwilling to return.

With nothing more to mention at present, we are grateful for your gracious attention.

Andrés Matijas, Gaspar Jiménez Vicente, Mateo Ramírez, Mateo Domingo, Marcos G., Pedro Domingo R., Felipe García D., Gaspar Carmelo Domingo, Felipe Paíz, Mateo Ramos Ramos, Sebastian Lucas G., Pedro Domingo
Guatemalan refugees in Chiapas, Mexico

Buses carry Guatemalan refugees home from Mexico where some 50,000 have lived in camps since the early 1980s (*above*), and a large number have mingled with the general population. Repatriation, the first choice of refugees and the international community that protects them, is often blocked by tenacious civil wars, many of which rage for decades and account for large numbers of casualties and human rights violations. Most Guatemalan refugees have not returned home because their land has been taken and because they fear they will be forced to join civil patrols and reside in model villages. *Background:* Protestors try to escape gunfire from the national police on the steps of the Metropolitan Cathedral, San Salvador, 1980.

Refugees settle among Ugandan livestock farmers in Ozuchinga settlement, across the border from their homeland in Rwanda, instead of in confining camps. Africa has been successful with its local settlement programs that foster self-sufficiency among its four million refugees.

SETTLING IN NEXT DOOR: AN AFRICAN ALTERNATIVE

I came by foot to Sudan in January 1984. I was desperate to save my life, and that is what drove me here. In Ethiopia I had no future, no hopes. I had been working for the government in the Relief and Rehabilitation Commission in Wollo province for fifteen years. Finally I was made the district supervisor. But the government thought I was a member of the Tigray People's Liberation Front. The Dergue is suspicious of everyone and is always seeking to capture sympathizers of one or the other of the liberation groups. I had no connection with any of the political groups, but innocence is no guarantee of safety. They threw me into prison. For six months I was in prison—I cannot talk about it, because it was so terrible. Of course they tortured me—they torture everyone who they suspect is part of the Tigray People's Liberation Front. Finally I was let out with a strong warning not to get involved with the counter-revolution.

Even though I was free, the police watched me everywhere. I was very afraid. Many of my friends were in prison, just like me, for many months. They were suspected of being anti-government. When they were let out, the police watched very carefully for any sign or proof to take them again. Many of my friends died this way. Just last week I heard they shot my uncle. At last, I decided it was too dangerous for me to stay, and so, to my great sadness, I left my old life and fled to Sudan.

I crossed the border near Kassala. In Kassala there are many refugees. I found a man, a refugee, who allowed me to stay at his house. I had no money, so I couldn't pay him anything. I didn't register as a refugee with the UNHCR or with the Commissioner of Refugees of Sudan (COR), because I knew nothing of them. Finally I found work with Médecins Sans Frontières, as an administrator. I kept that job for four months. I lived in the Médecins Sans Frontières workers' compound in Tukelabob. When Médecins Sans Frontières decided to move to Wad Kowli camp, I didn't want to go with them, because I knew nothing good about camps. I came to Tawawa instead, because I wanted to live in a settlement, not a camp.

By this time I had found friends, and I stayed with them. I registered with the Commissioner of Refugees and began to receive rations. In 1985 I was hired by the International Rescue Committee as the purchaser for hospital food. I did some interpreting for them, because I speak Arabic even though I cannot read or write it.

Many of my friends now are Sudanese. One, named Ali, became a friend when I was living in Tukelabob, but now he is working here in Tawawa, too. Through him I have met many Sudanese. You know, alcohol is illegal in Sudan, so my Sudanese friends come to my settlement where it is quiet to take a drink with me. And when I have trouble with other Sudanese, these friends help me. They come visit with me in Tawawa, and I visit them in Gedaref.

Every day I pass through the police check

"Though my life is no longer in danger, I do not feel at home in Sudan. Nothing is better here. If you are a refugee without papers, you are always frightened of being picked up."

between Tawawa and Gedaref on my way to work. I thought the police would give me trouble, but they know me, so there is no problem. I work from seven-thirty to one-thirty for the International Rescue Committee, and at three o'clock I teach kindergarden at the Swedish Save The Children Fund. I do this for one hour, for extra money.

Most days I go right home after work, because I have no money to spend on entertainment. I am living in my new wife's hut. I asked COR for a house when I moved here, but I never got one. When I first met my wife, she had a hut that COR built for her and her four children. She had a house but no money. I had a job, but no house. I felt I could not live alone, so we decided to live together. In our compound there are two houses and a kitchen, which I built with grass and sticks that COR gave me. There are twenty of us living here— my wife and her four children, her family, and my uncle and his family. Twenty in all. My wife and I support all of them. My wife makes bread and beer to sell to the locals.

Even though we have our own house, we have not been given land to farm. Some of our neighbors work the locals' fields when there is seasonal work to be done, and in this way they can make some money. Other refugees are given gardens, but we didn't manage to get one. Our compound is very narrow, and water is very expensive. We must pay $1.20 a barrel, and each week we need at least eight barrels for drinking and cooking.

Up until a year ago we got rations from the Sudanese government. But now we get none. Only the blind ones, and the old and the sick— the ones who cannot work—still get rations. There are many who depend on them. I think the government will start rations again for everyone. Some of the voluntary agencies help, too, like the Sudan Council of Churches and the International Rescue Committee.

Though my life is no longer in danger, I do not feel at home in Sudan. Nothing is better

here. The police will take you for no reason. If you are a refugee without papers, you are always frightened of being picked up. Many times they have stopped me. Last week they grabbed me and told me to put up my hands. They wanted to see if there was money in my pocket. I told them they had no right to do this. They took me to Gedaref jail. They insulted me, and they said, "Smell the earth." By this they meant, "Put your face in the dirt and smell that it is not your land." When they found out that I was an International Rescue Committee employee, it went better for me. They knew IRC would come for me. There was no reason for this arrest. They just wanted money.

At least in the Gedaref market I have no trouble. I go to the same merchants every day, and they know me very well. They treat me the same as a brother. But if another refugee goes to the market, he must face higher prices. He is always insulted. The merchants call him "Abyssinian," which has a very bad meaning.

It is very hard for me to think about my future. I would go home immediately if there were no political problems. In Ethiopia I lived on one job, and I had time to enjoy my friends. I had my own house. It was made from wood and had three rooms with electricity. And I have a wife and children there. But the situation in Ethiopia is very difficult and will take a long, long time to solve. I don't think about going back. It is too complicated.

I hope sometimes for resettlement, but I have no relatives in America, so there is really no chance. You see, I cannot have a stable plan. Everything depends on the government in Sudan. I am not in my own hands. I am in the government's hands. And the government is not stable, not at all stable. I cannot say, "I will do this, and this, and this in the next three years." I cannot plan. I cannot know what is next.

BIRHANI PAULOS, Tigrayan
locally settled in Sudan

Rwandese refugees *(above)*, settled locally in Tanzania, use seed and tools provided by the United Nations High Commissioner for Refugees to cultivate fields and become self-sufficient. Some 200,000 African refugees benefit by living in local settlements, loosely knit communities that sometimes merge with established villages. *Background:* Milton Obote's army strafes a field protecting insurgent forces in Uganda. Long-standing military conflicts throughout Africa keep millions of Africans on the move. When violence subsides, Africans spontaneously return home, usually to be forced out when the next wave of war erupts.

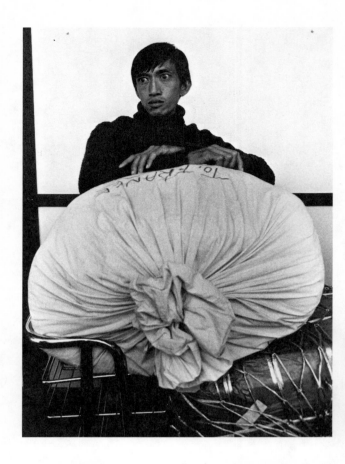

A Cambodian refugee waits at Charles DeGaulle airport, en route from a camp in Thailand to his new home in Paris. Of the 14 million refugees under international protection, one percent are accepted for resettlement in third countries, for many the last chance to begin a new life.

MOVING TO A NEW COUNTRY: THE ONE-PERCENT OPTION

The total area of Pulau Bidong was about five square kilometers, of which only one kilometer was suitable for living—the rest being too steep. This island was rented by the UNHCR, and it was one of six refugee camps in Malaysia. Generally, all the boat people were allowed to enter the camp, and were given a boat number. After that, a photograph of each person was taken and handed to the resettlement delegations according to boat number. We were required to fill in documents, and the Executive Committee of the camp showed us very clearly how to apply to the UNHCR for resettlement in a third country.

When we arrived on the island, it was summer. The Malaysian climate was much hotter than the Vietnamese, especially between ten o'clock in the morning and four o'clock in the afternoon. Sometimes it was absolutely still, with not the slightest wisp of a breeze, and then we felt as if we were standing in an oven. Yet the island was our refuge. When the Malaysian premier announced that he was ordering all refugees who had not been chosen for resettlement back out to sea, we froze. My parents-in-law became so worried they were sick, and the morale of the people sank very low. We asked

"We dreamt of going to America, and learning trades, and sponsoring our families. But our waiting time got longer and longer. We swore at the slowness of the selection committees."

those friends who were leaving for other countries to post letters for us when they left the island, but we waited forever without receiving replies. The disappointment and the disillusion seemed to envelop me, and sometimes I broke and vented my anger on my children without any reason.

In a few months the population of the island increased by about 10,000. Many people had an unfounded fear that the island would sink into the sea and disappear completely with the weight of all the people. I felt as if the planet had stopped and had forgotten about us. One day seemed to be one year. Yet, nothing happened, we weren't cast off the island, for as my husband said, the Malaysians were only playing a psychological game to pressure other countries to accept more refugees for resettlement.

When we had filled out our application forms, we had hesitated in our choice of country. This was vital, for when the document was completed, it was given to the delegate of the country concerned. Most of the refugees wanted to go to Australia, for it was known as a new country with a lot of land and few people, and we knew that the job situation there was better than in other countries, while the climate was more temperate. Yet at that time the selection made by the Australian delegate was very strict. The majority of people were not approved. Therefore, at the time we applied, we decided to divide ourselves into three families—one of eight, one of four, and one of two. We chose our second preference as America, for America had priorities which would favor our family of eight, since one of the family, my sister-in-law, was the widow of a man who had fallen fighting in the war. We all prayed that she would be chosen so my old parents-in-law could leave the island. If they left first, then later they would be able to sponsor us.

To kill time we dreamt a lot. To run from our worry for the future we dreamt. We said that later on, if we were allowed to go to Australia, I could work to save money to sponsor all of our family out. We would contribute our money to buying a boat to ply the South China Sea, and rescue all the refugees bobbing on the waves. We dreamt of going to America, and learning trades, and sponsoring our families out. But our waiting time got longer and longer, and there seemed no hope, and we swore at the slowness of the selection committees, and we waited, and concentrated every time they announced the names of the people chosen, and we found that our names were not there.

July 10 was one of the happiest and also one of the saddest days of my life. The two smaller families among us were accepted by Australia, and our neighbours shared our joys, and my mother-in-law cried with happiness, and my father-in-law was speechless, and it was as if our two children could understand this joy, for they were jumping up and down on a bed. The lunch that day tasted so good, although the food was the same—chicken and canned sardines. Exactly a month later, our names appeared on the list of people allowed to leave the island, and we were asked to prepare to go. When the weather improved, we were to leave straight away.

For the first time ever, after five months on Pulau Bidong, I found that time passed quickly. We felt a particular affinity and love for the rest of our family and pity for our parents, so old, so frail, who had to stay back waiting to go to America. Nobody could stop the tears. My niece just clung to our smaller son and kissed him continuously. My mother-in-law loved us so much that she could not bear to see us leaving: she could not embrace us for the last time. She ran to hide, and cried aloud, and told us just to leave. When we left and looked back, we saw her waving. Everything now is just memory.

The boat left the island at five o'clock in the afternoon, with the sun rays hot about me.

For the first time, that was loving.

HAN-HAI-VAN, Vietnamese,
Pulau Bidong camp, Malaysia

A Cambodian (*above*) bids farewell to officials at Khao I Dang camp, Thailand, the major processing center for refugees from Southeast Asia. During the five to seven years a refugee normally remains in a camp, officials conduct interviews to select likely candidates for successful resettlement, according to specific criteria and quotas. Nearly 655,000 refugees from Laos, Vietnam, and Cambodia have passed through Thailand for resettlement since the late 1970s. Thailand agreed to accept its displaced neighbors only on the condition that third countries would invite them to resettle. *Background:* The Pol Pot regime waged genocide against the Cambodian people from 1975 to 1979, killing millions and destroying the countryside, including Phom Penh, the capital. Those who survived carry with them the trauma of devastation into their new lives.

Palestinian refugees flee during the 1967 Arab-Israeli war. Living in camps has become a permanent way of life for 793,000 Palestinians, some of whom have been under United Nations protection since 1948.

GOING NOWHERE: THE HOPELESS WHO REMAIN IN LIMBO

I was born in 1943 in Berziet, ten miles north of Jerusalem, four years before the war. So I was four years old when the refugees first came to our town when the tragedy started. A year later, my mother told me to put black sheets over the windows and to stay close to home because the streets might no longer be safe.

When the refugees came she opened our house to them and made them welcome, telling them, "Stay here. This may be your home until you can go back to your own." Five families stayed with us. Our house was very large, but it had only one room. There must have been twenty-five or thirty people in addition to my own family; and some people even had to live on our roof during the summer when it was very hot. At first my sisters and I were upset, and we kept saying to our mother, "But where shall we sleep? You gave them our beds and we are tired." She whispered to us, "Be easy, it will only be for a week or so, at the most a month, and everyone will go home again." We had to sleep on the floor in a corner beside our mother, without a bed and privacy for four years! When I asked my mother, "Why do these people have to stay in our house?," she told me, "Because Israel took away their lands and they have no homes."

I felt bitterness because of that, and anger. I felt homeless, too, even in my own home, because the refugees who lived with us were oc-

"They came with nothing, with only the feeling that they would soon be able to return home. They had all kept their house keys with them."

cupying my house. I knew we were in the middle of a bad problem, but I didn't really understand why it had to happen to us, changing our lives so suddenly, so completely.

It wasn't as bad for me, of course, as it was for those people from the first part of Palestine to be occupied. They came with nothing, with only the feeling that they would soon be able to return home. They had all kept their house keys with them. My brother, who had come to us from Jaffa, would say to me, "Do not lose the key to my house, whatever you do. We will need it when we go home to Jaffa." It was kept on top of a cupboard, and I would go to look at it from time to time, and think of the beautiful city I had never seen. The city I would never see. One of the refugees had left her baby on the bed, and when she had had to flee so quickly, she grabbed up the pillow instead of her baby and ran away. She would cry and cry and say to us, "I want to go back for my baby! What if he has been hurt? I must go back!" It is a picture I cannot forget, that woman sobbing so helplessly for her child.

After a time we were under the jurisdiction of the Jordanian government, which separated the refugees into large groups and gave them land to build tent camps in Palestine, Jordan, or Lebanon. They lived there one, two, three years. After a while, no one could imagine how long it would be before they would be allowed to go home. Many organizations began to give refugees food and milk, but you can't imagine what it was like in those tent camps in winter! Small children were without shoes, without enough food, freezing. They grew up feeling they wanted their homeland back, the gardens they had played in, the life they had once known.

In 1948 eighty percent of the Palestinians were forced to give up their lands. Even at that time we were not as understanding about the refugees and their suffering as we should have been. We still looked down on them as second-class citizens. They were the refugees while we were the owners of the land they were camping on. We could not then believe that we would soon be refugees, too. But then, in 1967, there was the tragedy of the Six Days' War, and all of our land was occupied. All of us were refugees then. No one knew that once we had left our city we could never return for our furniture or money or whatever else we possesed.

NUHA NAFAL, Palestinian living in the
United States

Baqaa camp, Jordan, is one of the largest camps housing Palestinian refugees. Some 793,000 of the 2.3 million Palestinian refugees live in 61 camps in Jordan, Lebanon, Gaza Strip, the West Bank, and Syria. Temporary tents, which originally housed Palestinian and Jewish people who fled when Palestine was partitioned in 1947, evolved into mud-brick or concrete-block homes for Palestinian refugees. *Background:* a photograph of Jerusalem, the symbol of homeland to Palestinians and Jews, hangs on a bombed wall in Lebanon. Since 1948 major conflicts in 1956, 1967, 1973, and 1982, and the uprising in the occupied territories that began in 1987, have kept the area in a state of constant war.

THE WALL OF RESISTANCE

les Français d'abord!

Votez Jean-Marie Le Pen

VU LE CANDIDAT

Front d'Opposition Nationale pour l'Europe des Patries.
11, rue Bernouilli. 75008 PARIS.

IRANI ARE A DISGR TO ISL

Iranians are a Disgrace to ISLAM

The Wall of Resistance: *First row:* "The French Come First," poster of ultra-right leader Jean Marie Le Pen; "France Belongs to the French," scrawled on a Paris building; "Jewish Joke, Turkish Joke, Auschwitz," sign on a West Berlin car; anti-Pakistani sentiments on a London slum building. *Second row:* American anti-Iranian demonstrations, Washington, D.C.; "Miami News" cartoon; "Keep Sweden Swedish" banner in Stockholm; anti-Pakistani joke on hood of Norwegian car. *Third row:* bumper sticker on a truck in Biloxi, Mississippi; racist graffiti on a London house; "Foreigners Out" on a Bonn building; pig's trotters with National Front insignia left at a Bengali's home, London. *Right page:* National Front campaign poster, London.

MISSISSIPPI NOV 80 FN9 376 *the Hospitality State* JACKSON

SAVE YOUR SHRIMP INDUSTRY
GET RID OF VIETNAMESE
CONTACT YOUR LOCAL CONGRESSMAN

National Front demonstrators march in London protesting Great Britain's immigration policy.
Overleaf: the West's xenophobic attitude toward asylum seekers is expressed in a barrage of graffiti, slogans, and posters.

STOP immigration
Britons first in jobs and housing
National Front

STOP immi...
NF
STOP integration
START repatriation
National Front

3.
SHUTTING THE DOORS: REFUGEE GO HOME

MATTHEW PARKER ST.

the British

Your last chance...

The NATIONAL FRONT

enwitz
renwitz
chwitz

FIT FOUR
PIGS
& ASIAN
SWINES

BEVARA
SVERIGE
SVENSKT

UNDER DETTE PANSER ER DET IKKE MOTOR,
MEN TI TOPPTRIMEDE PAKISTANERE

VAHL

78

BEDFO

EN KLOKE KLEPTOMAN?
EN HEVENDAHL PYROMAN?

WE SIND GRÖMSET
DA MAN
KVINNEN
?

DREP SMÅ BARN DB 46

DER
NAZIS

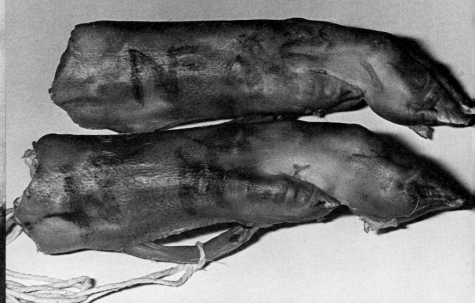

I realized my days of freedom were numbered and that I would have to act immediately. I learned by word of mouth that, with a great deal of money, it would be possible to be smuggled to a safe harbor and escape my fate in Iran. I thought I could go the United States, where I have two sisters with permanent resident status. The prevailing wisdom in Iran, however, was that Canada was a better prospect for political asylum. I had been told that without valid travel documents, the U.S. authorities would send me back to Iran immediately. I therefore took out a substantial amount of my savings and set out to find my way to Canada.

First, I traveled to the Iran-Pakistan border, where for a fee of 80,000 *toumans* (about $10,000) I was smuggled across by a friend's uncle. He assured my passage to Karachi, where I was taken to an Iranian's house. I stayed there for three or four days, during which time I procured a forged Iranian passport, entry and exit permits for Pakistan, an Indian visa, and an airline ticket to Bombay. Although I was not happy resorting to forged documents, I knew there was no other way to escape. Time was clearly of the essence, and once I had decided upon my destination, I could not afford to linger.

Once I got to Bombay, my next step was to get a ticket to North America. I had heard that there were two smugglers in Bombay, one an Iranian and one an Afghan. When I inquired about the Iranian, I learned he had been arrested. I went to the Afghan, Mehdi. When I asked him for a ticket and documents to get to Canada, Mehdi discouraged me, saying I had a greater chance of being arrested at a stopover on a Canadian flight than I did if I went to the United States. He asked if I knew anyone in the U.S. Hearing about my two sisters, Mehdi told me I should telephone them and have them meet me at the airport with a lawyer, who could vouch for me and help me in my asylum

Swiss border police round up Yugoslavs who attempted to enter the country without proper documentation. Since the mid-1970s, western nations, including the United States and Canada, under the pressures of a weakened world economy and increasing numbers of people seeking asylum, have tightened requirements and created deterrents aimed at stopping asylum seekers from receiving protection in the West. Virtually every western nation is revising its asylum and immigration laws, in spite of the fact that ninety-five percent of the people seeking asylum remain in third world countries.

application. He assured me that because I had relatives there, my application would most likely be approved. Moreover, he noted my arrival would coincide with Christmas, and that everyone in New York is especially nice at that time.

I bought a ticket to New York and a passport from Mehdi which had originally been issued to an Afghan woman whose photo and date of birth had been obliterated and my own substituted. This passport cost me $1,800. I called my sisters to arrange for them to meet my flight. Though I was unable to reach them, I realized I had to leave the country anyway.

Mehdi accompanied me to the airport; since he spoke Hindi, he handled the departure forms, talked to the airline personnel, and made sure I got to the gate. The flight departed Bombay on December 25 and landed first in Dublin, then in London. When the plane stopped briefly to refuel and pick up passengers, I remained in the departure lounge. Mehdi had instructed me to destroy my travel papers after leaving London. I did so. I hid in the lavatory when arrival cards were distributed and collected, so my undocumented passage went unnoticed.

When the plane landed in New York on December 26, I disembarked last. I saw a few Indians and a Bangladeshi ahead of me being questioned. I realized I, too, would be questioned. I approached an immigration officer, and he soon discovered I had no documents. He sent for a Persian-speaking Swissair employee who translated for me. I was asked where I was from and who had sent me. Again, following Mehdi's instructions, I said I didn't know. Two Air India employees came to search my bags for documents. I was fingerprinted and asked to sign a form.

MOHAMMED REZA NOORI, Iranian businessman, detained in New York

We were deported from the United States to Korea on March 29. The next day Korean Airlines took us to Taiwan and then to Hong

A Lebanese asylum seeker, being deported by immigration authorities from Tegel airport, Berlin, breaks down and pleads to remain in Germany instead of being returned to Lebanon. Deportation is a last resort used by countries to control increasing numbers of asylum seekers. West German asylum applications increased from under 9,000 in 1970 to over 100,000 in 1980. Since 1987 visas have been required for admission to most European countries, and governments are levying fines up to $2,000 against airlines carrying people traveling without proper documents.

Kong. Hong Kong refused us and sent us back to Korea. The Koreans then sent us to Sri Lanka and told the Sri Lankan authorities that we should be sent on to Afghanistan, because the U.S. State Department had instructed them to do this. The Sri Lankan government refused to accept us and stated that sending us back was against all human rights principles. So Korean Airlines took us to Saudi Arabia.

> AMANULLAH OBAIDI,
> Afghan refugee in orbit

As soon as we arrived at Heathrow Airport, my husband was taken away from us. He struggled and was hit in the face. We did not know what was happening. We thought we had come to freedom. We told them we had been badly treated in Iraq and Iran and had had to escape.

In the night an interpreter came to our room in the detention center, but we were too scared to talk and were very tired. We were searched naked and interviewed, but we were not sure what information we should give.

We were interviewed, separately, again. Then

Right: To avoid detention in a federal center in Puerto Rico, a Haitian jumps from the plane carrying him out of Miami. Between 1971 and 1981, approximately 35,000 to 45,000 Haitian boat people arrived in the United States. Many were arrested and detained pending final determination of their right to asylum. *Below:* members of the Hong Kong border patrol capture Chinese aliens as they attempt to cross the fenced border into Hong Kong. Detained for twenty-four hours, the 50,000 who try to make it through nightly are questioned and usually returned to Canton.

an officer told us we must return to Yugoslavia. But we said they would send us back to Iran or Iraq.

The baby cried, but I was not allowed to feed her. An officer put her arm tightly around my neck, and I was sick. Two officers held my husband. We were very frightened, and the children were hungry and crying.

I was very upset. Two men and two women officials handcuffed me with my hands behind my back and straps around my feet. My husband was handcuffed too. The officials said, "If we don't restrain you, you might try to kill yourselves."

SAYRAN RASHID,
Iraqi Kurd, detained in London

I felt I could not be honest at the asylum hearing, and I did not feel at liberty to say so. All questions the judge asked me had a double meaning: the answers could have been both "Yes" and "No." Everything in the courtroom was meant to frighten me, to intimidate me, to humiliate me, to throw me out of the country. It seems to me that with these kinds of proceedings, it doesn't matter whether one goes with or without a lawyer.

Guatemalan detained in Boston

In my country, I was a shepherd. I was outside all day. Now I am cooped up inside, and I can't stand it. After twenty-five years of suffering, I end up in an American jail. I thought I would find freedom as a refugee in this country, but my suffering continues. I came here to hide from persecution. This is beyond my limit. Here my heart beats fast, and my body shakes. Being here is like a bad dream.

ROBERT GARDENER, South African,
detained in New York

Dear Readers, Gentlemen, Civilian, and Military Authorities,

For the last few months we have been im-

Above: Sikh businessmen, who arrived "illegally" by boat via Germany from India, obscure their identity at a Toronto press conference. *Below:* Seventy Iranians, traveling on forged visas from Turkey to Sweden, are intercepted by immigration officials in the Stockholm airport. Many Iranian refugees use an "underground railroad" to leave Iran, paying up to $4,000 to agents who often abandon them in desolate places.

Haitians fight boredom and alienation at Camp Krome detention center, outside Miami. Beginning in 1981, Haitians arriving by boat in southern Florida without proper entry documents were detained at Camp Krome, a former Nike missile base in the Everglades swamp. There are seven U.S. detention centers with a capacity of more than 4,000 persons. Detainees, isolated from family and friends, find it difficult to obtain adequate legal representation or social support. Some Haitians are confined for over two years.

Kemal Cemal Altun, a Turk seeking political asylum in Germany, is led into a West Berlin hearing room *(above)*. Nervously surveying the room, he notices an open window. (continued on following page)

prisoned without knowing what outcome our fates would have.

One day around 4 PM we women were all gathered at the sound of whistles. We spent a day and a night awaiting our fate, after having been tagged with a plastic ID bracelet. After that we were made to parade nude in front of men and women. We were spashed, badly treated. Stripped of our clothes and belongings, we were made to sit in a room where we were to spend the night. The room was like a wake, where sad songs were being sung. At that moment, an enormous chill would run down the spine. Around 5 AM we were jammed in a bus which was to drive us to the airport. This is how we left Miami for Puerto Rico.

When we left Miami, we were led to believe we were only going to Puerto Rico for a few days. And until now we have been suffering for eight months without knowing why. Each day we hear only one thing: those who wish to return to Haiti can give their names.

Our situation is pitiful. We have been locked up behind barbed wire from Miami to Puerto Rico. The days are always the same for us. We don't know what the date is. Sometimes we are hungry and cannot eat.

Now we cannot stand it anymore. It is too much. If we have not been freed by the end of November, a good number of us are going to commit suicide. Because we have sworn to die in the United States.

Haitian women detained at
Fort Allen, Puerto Rico

Today at 2 PM, I had to go to the Lucerne police. I don't speak German very well, so I asked a friend of mine who speaks English to accompany me. We met at the police station. The officer who accepted my petition for asylum a few months ago was there. He sent my friend away; he wanted to talk to me alone, and he thought I spoke enough German. He explained, "You have to enter a hospital. Your health is very bad." I responded, "My doctor never talked to me about this." "Another doctor did," he answered. Then I had to go into another room and wait. There was a table, a chair, and some newspapers. Bare walls with cement and graffiti. Someone had written in Turkish, "I was in Switzerland. Have to return to Turkey." Below was a name and a date. I remembered similar cell walls in Turkey. Two men picked me up and took me to a police vehicle. I guess they were policemen. Both were armed, about six feet tall. "Where are we going?" I asked. "To the hospital," they responded. We went back to the hotel and up to my room. I had to pack everything. A friend who shares the room with me wanted to know where I was going. "Probably to the hospital," I said. "Call when you arrive there," he responded.

I didn't trust the policemen. "Will they take me to a hospital?" I asked myself. We went back with my things to the car. One policeman was up in front; one was in back with me. They brought me to the district police. In a large cell I had to sit and make a list of my personal belongings. Then I filled out a form asking for details about myself in Turkish. There was a question, "Why have you been arrested?" I didn't know the answer. I asked the policeman. He thought I could put down a question mark. At five in the afternoon, they took me to the Central Police station. There I was put in a cell. Again a table, a chair, a bed, a toilet. Way up on top, a small window with bars. Before they locked me up I asked, "How long do I have to stay?" "Perhaps until tomorrow." "Why am I here?" Silence.

I was alone. I was confused. I was disturbed, full of questions. Why am I being treated like a criminal? Would they take me back to Turkey? At 5:30 a guard opened the little hole in the cell door. "We'll bring you food." I couldn't eat. I was full of fear.

There was a noise that woke me up the next morning at 5:15. "At six o'clock, you have to be ready for departure." I ate bread and cheese, but I didn't touch the soup. I swallowed my medicine, and I waited. "What will happen to me today?" Then they brought me back to the police depot. "Where are you taking me?" "To Germany." "To Germany?"

I remembered the dispute I had some

months ago when I put in my petition. Then the police in charge of foreigners insisted I had been in Germany. I told them this was wrong. The police insisted, "We know you. We have your fingerprints. It's clear you have lived in Germany." I wondered, when they brought me to Germany, if they would then take me on to Turkey? "Can I telephone?" I asked. "I want to tell my friends where I am, what has happened." They said no, I couldn't.

They put me in handcuffs, and led me to the station. People stopped to look at me, and I was ashamed. Am I a murderer? A thief? What have I done? Nothing. Nothing at all. I sit on the train. "What will happen in Basel?" I can't imagine, and I can't think any more.

Shortly before the train arrives, the police take my watch, my pen, and my paper. Again handcuffs. Again into the police waiting room. Other men are sitting there. They put us in a vehicle for prisoners. At the police station, we make a stop. After ten minutes, a sixteen-year-old boy is added to the car. We start driving again. "Where are you going?" I ask a man, and he says, "Back to Yugoslavia, and you?" "I don't know," I say. We get near to the airport. "Will they send me back to Turkey?" My thoughts are racing. "What can I do?" I will try to flee from the room with the bars. I will try to flee, because in Ankara at the airport they will arrest me immediately. Then they will torture me.

Now they take the young boy away. So am I

155

going to Germany? We continue to drive. Then they stop and bring me to the German customs agent at the station, and they say, ''This one belongs to you.'' They hand over a package with my documents and my personal belongings, and now I am with German police. The German policemen read my documents. They want to know my address in Germany. ''I don't have an address there. I have never been to Germany,'' I repeat. Again, take down all my information. They don't believe me about where I was born. ''I can prove that based on my papers I did not lie about my place of birth.'' They get very nervous. They telephone. Then I have to tell them how I got to Switzerland. Again, another long telephone call, this one to Hannover. Then everything is cleared up. The police have mixed me up with a Turkish national of the same name and date of birth but a different place of birth. This man lives in Hannover. ''You're right,'' they say. ''What do you want to do now?'' ''I want to go back to Lucerne. That's where I have my friends, my doctor, and my petition.''

Between 2:30 and 1 PM they write out the documents for the Swiss police. Then they take my fingerprints and photograph me. Finally they give me back to the Swiss who are very surprised to see me. They promise to take me back to Lucerne. In the waiting room of the station I wait in the same cell in the postal compartment until five o'clock. I'm totally exhausted. This time we're heading towards Lu-

cerne. In Lucerne, again the handcuffs, again the people. We drive back to the district police. They take off my handcuffs. They give me my belongings. ''Now you're free. Shall we bring you back to the hotel?'' ''No thank you,'' I say, ''I know my way.''

Turkish asylum seeker in Lucerne

I first heard about Sanctuary when I was living in Mexico. For a year and a half I had been looking for help, for *real* help, because I was living underground, always at risk. When I left Guatemala, I left without money, without any idea of where to go. I will never forget that when I left my father and my mother each gave me one thing. My father told me, ''Son, I don't have anything to give you, any money, anything.'' So he took off his hat and put it on my head. My mother had a very cheap watch, and she took the watch from her arm and she put it on my arm. Once when I was caught by Mexican immigration, I offered the agent my hat and watch because I didn't have any money. They were the price for my release.

While I was living underground, a Mexican came to me, because he had heard I was looking for help. He told me that in the United States there was a movement of churches concerned about the situation in Central America. They knew many refugees were being sent back to Salvador and Guatemala, who were now dead. These congregations were offering shelter, legal help, and medical help for refugees.

"There was a question, 'Why have you been arrested?' I didn't know the answer. I asked the policeman. He thought I could put down a question mark."

Help was possible for me, my wife, and little daughter.

At the time, I was nearer to the border of Mexico and Guatemala, so I had to cross the whole country to get to the U.S.-Mexican border. It was a long trip. The Mexican gave us money for shelter, busfare, and things like that. He didn't advise us in political terms, but he told us how to act on the trip, and how to talk with a Mexican accent. He advised us to trust him and the other Sanctuary workers. Even though he was traveling with us, we were always mistrusting, because we didn't know him or his background. In the meantime we were hoping he was good.

Crossing the border was hard because we had to cross alone—Sanctuary people told us what to do but they waited for us inside the

U.S. On our first attempt we were arrested, and I was in immigration jail in Arizona for a couple of days. Well I lied to them; I told them I was Mexican. They deported me to Mexico. Once back in Mexico, I got help to cross the border again. I crossed on foot, and a Sanctuary worker drove me to Arizona.

In Phoenix we were helped a lot by Sister Darlene. Since she is a nun we felt good being with her. She knew that the First United Methodist Church in Germantown, Pennsylvania, was offering Sanctuary for our family. We left Phoenix and on the way across country we met many people. We stayed at many houses and churches—when I say churches I mean congregations—of Jewish people, Quakers, Christians.

Fifteen days after we arrived in Philadelphia the First United Methodist Church prepared a

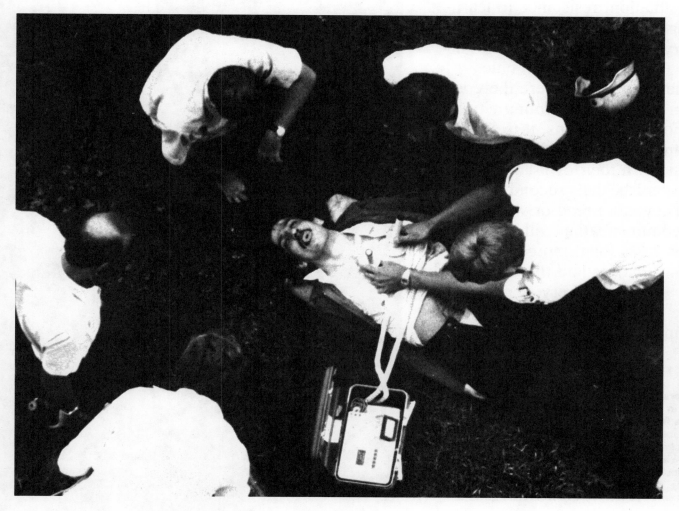

Opposite page and left: Alton's desperation, which has grown in the months of waiting for a judgment, and his fear that his application for political asylum will be refused, propel him toward the window and his death six floors below. German officials claim the average period for a case to be determined is six months. Voluntary agencies indicate the process can take up to three years.

welcoming service for us. At first we lived in the church for a couple of months, until a Methodist minister and his family offered us an apartment, where we are now living. During that time we were always in public. We had speaking engagements, because they gave us the opportunity to talk about the atrocities my people are suffering. The time passed this way: we met more people; we started English, we went to meetings and reunions with friends. We didn't stay hidden, but we didn't give our phone number to many people, and we didn't say where we were living.

Sanctuary lawyers helped us apply for political asylum. It took more than one year and thousands of hours of work to get the application in order. They tried to help us live in healthier conditions, because when we arrived, we were sick, skinny, weak.

Being in the U.S. is even harder than being in Mexico. You face a new language and strange food. Your eyes suffer seeing the system, the luxury in this country, the easy way things are done. You get an upset stomach and diahrrea, and you vomit thinking of the uncertainty. Besides suffering, there is resistance to accepting the new situation, resistance to learning the new language. Refugees are mostly people from the countryside, and they confront difficulties when they move to American cities. Some of them come from areas where there is no electricity. Even if they come from a city, it's a big change. For Guatemalans, it is extremely hard to come here. Sixty percent of the population is Indian, with their own languages. They don't speak Spanish, their second language, very well. They can't read or write, so they have trouble communicating with North Americans, and this gives them more headaches. Sometimes the headaches and the stomach upset take years to go away. Every single refugee suffers.

Guatemalan in Sanctuary, Philadelphia

Salvadorans in Sanctuary worship at a church in Chicago. The Sanctuary movement began in Tucson in 1980 in response to U.S. policy of not accepting Central Americans for asylum. More than 400 churches and synagogues provide shelter for illegal aliens and assist them in obtaining legal status and in returning home when possible. Leaders of the Sanctuary movement say the aliens they help are fleeing political oppression. The U.S. government insists they are economic migrants trying to better their standard of living. Of the 750,000 Salvadorans in the U.S., 528, or 2.6 percent were granted political asylum from June 1983 to September 1986.

Malians survey the rubble of their living compound in St. Denis, France. Disturbed that housing was being constructed for the 300 Malian workers, members of the communist party attacked the complex. While Europe has worked toward a relatively generous social service system regarding housing, the right to work, and access to the legal process, because of a weakened economic climate, nationals fear their rights to jobs and other services are being threatened by foreigners.

SOME FACTS YOU SHOULD KNOW: XENOPHOBIA IN THE FIRST WORLD

Number of people who sought political asylum in western Europe between 1976–86: 750,000
In 1986: 198,200
In 1987: 178,400

Percentage of western Europe's population this represents: under 0.5

By country in 1987: Germany 57,400; France 24,800; Sweden 18,100; Netherlands 13,450; Austria 11,400; Italy 11,050; Switzerland 10,900; Norway 8,600; Greece 6,950; Belgium 6,000; United Kingdom 4,500; Denmark 2,750; Spain 2,500

Percentage of "unfounded" asylum-applications in the West: 10–15

Percentage of asylum seekers throughout the world who settle permanently in country where they first arrive: 50 plus

Average amount charged by "racketeers" for forged tickets and documents needed to reach the West from Iran or El Salvador: $2,000 to $5,000 plus

Number of countries requiring entry visas for specific groups of incoming foreigners: 12

Countries that fine airlines for carrying passengers without proper documentation: United Kingdom 1,000 pounds; Holland 2,000 guilders; United States $1,000; West Germany DM 2,000

Length of time it takes to complete asylum proceeding: 6 months to 7 years

Countries that allow applicant to work while waiting for an asylum hearing: United Kingdom and Canada (after six months), France, The Netherlands, United States (non-frivolous claims)

UNITED KINGDOM

Asylum applications made in 1985: 4,859

Number of persons granted asylum in the United Kingdom in the first six months of 1986: 454
In 1987: 2

Percentage of Britain's total population represented by the number of asylum seekers who arrived between 1984–86: .2

Average length of time for Home Office to decide on individual asylum application: 1 year

Percentage since 1980 of people seeking asylum in the United Kingdom who come from Iran, Iraq, Sri Lanka, Poland, Ghana, Ethiopia, or Uganda: 80

Number of "collective accommodations" for detaining asylum seekers in Britain as of April 1987: 100 plus

Decrease in number of persons arriving weekly without proper documentation since passage of 1987 Carrier Liability Act: from 60 to 12

Reported deportations in early 1970s: under 500 a year
In early 1980s: 2,000–2,500

WEST GERMANY

Number of applications for asylum received by West Germany in 1975: 9,494
In 1986: 99,650
In 1987: 57,400

Percentage drop (presumed to be because of effective deterrents): 58

Percentage increase of people seeking political asylum in Berlin from 1984 to 1985 (before border restrictions): 109

Number of asylum seekers coming through East Germany into West Berlin between January and July 1986: 20–22,000

During same period in 1987 after restrictions: 3,500

SWITZERLAND

Number of people seeking asylum in Switzerland in 1976: 856

In 1986: 8,500

In 1987: 10,900

Percentage of individuals who sought asylum in Switzerland in 1986 who are Turkish: 50

Percentage of people approved in Switzerland for the first eight months of 1984: 16.1

For the same time period in 1987: 9

SCANDINAVIA

Number of asylum applications in Norway in 1984: 300

In 1986: 2,700

In 1987: 8,600

Number of asylum requests received by Denmark in 1983: 800

In 1986: 9,300

In 1987: 2,750

Number of refugees estimated by Danish citizens to be in Denmark: 100,000 to 1,000,000

Actual number admitted since the Danish Refugee Council started in 1956: 30,000

Percentage of Sweden's total population represented by asylum seekers who arrived there between 1985–86: .5

FRANCE

Number of asylum seekers 1986: 23,400

In 1987: 24,800

Percentage of asylum seekers accepted in 1982: 74

In 1986: 40

In 1987: 32.5

Percentage granted asylum from the following countries: Turkey: 32.8; Angola: 6.8; Haiti: 11; Chile: 82.2; Vietnam: 92.3; Cambodia: 87.6; China: 0.07; Sri-Lanka: 23.20; Iran: 69.3

Percentage of Tamil asylum seekers rejected by France in 1987: 95

CANADA

Number of asylum applications made in 1985: 8,374

In 1986: 18,283

In 1987: 25,944

Applicants granted asylum in 1987: 942, or 1 in 6 people

Political asylum applications pending in Canada at end of 1986: 14,000

At end of 1987: 44,000

UNITED STATES

Number of applications for asylum received by the U.S. each year before 1975: 200

Percentage of refugees admitted from non-communist countries or outside the Middle East from 1981–87: .2

Asylum cases filed with the U.S. Immigration and Naturalization Service in 1985: 16,622

In 1986: 18,889

In 1987: 26,107

In 1988: 60,736

Percentage of asylum requests approved by INS since 1980: 25

According to nationality through March 1988: China 85.7; Ethiopia 77.7; Iran 77.5; Romania 76.9; Vietnam 75; Uganda 61.5; Nicaragua 74.9; Afghanistan 44; Czechoslovakia 40; Poland 39.1; El Salvador 3.2; Guatemala 2.7

Percentage increase of refugee admission ceilings for East Europe and Soviet Union from 1987–88: 100

Number of Haitians stopped on high seas between September 1981 and September 1988 by U.S. Coast Guard and sent back to Haiti without asylum hearing: 16,000 plus

Number given asylum hearing: 4

Percentage of INS officers who have training in refugee and asylum issues: 2

Number of INS border guards in 1986: 2,900

In 1987: 4,000

Undocumented aliens apprehended in 1986: 1,692,544

In 1987: 1,157,030

Percentage decrease: 31.6

Approval rate for persons entering the U.S. legally in 1986: 38

For those entering illegally: 1.6

Percentage of Salvadorans seeking asylum who were returned home without asylum hearings October 1979–September 1983: 66

Number of detention centers in the United States: 9

People detained: 3,000 plus

Number who have legitimate claims to refugee status: 1,000

Number of children held in detention in the course of one year: 10,000

Number held on any given day: 150–200

Cost per day in 1985 to incarcerate an alien in a detention center: $19.27 (El Paso, Texas) to $132.75 (Boston)

Average stay in a detention center before a case is heard: 2–12 months

Range of bond required to be released from detention: $500–10,000

Number of cities declared cities of refuge for Central Americans: 28

Number of Sanctuary congregations in the United States: 435

Number of people who have been in Sanctuary: 1,000–2,000

Percentage of Americans who believe immigration levels should be decreased: 49

Percentage who believe immigrants "take more than they give": 64

NO PLACE TO GO: CONTROLLING WHO GETS IN

BILL FRELICK

Refugees are inconvenient. Their concern is not for order, systems, or bureaucracies, nor for the general welfare. Their concern, rather, is for survival—their own and that of their families.

Governments, on the other hand, have competing concerns: the sovereignty of borders, relations with neighboring countries, controlling immigration, promoting ruling ideologies, placating public opinion. If offering asylum to a refugee is consonant with those concerns, a government might come to his aid. If, however, the government cannot see a benefit in terms of its own interests, there is little incentive to pay the costs associated with extending protection to the refugee.

This is a delicate game in terms of public relations. Governments want to be perceived as good guys; they normally use the language of humanitarianism to explain why they grant asylum to refugees. It is difficult, however, for them to explain why some refugees are rejected. The tendency, it turns out, is to rationalize rejection by saying the others are not really refugees at all—people with a "well-founded fear of persecution" if returned to their homeland. They are "economic migrants" or "illegal aliens" undeserving of the government's generosity. They haven't waited their turn; they haven't obeyed the rules; their travel documents are not in order.

This rationalization for denying asylum rests, in part, on a simplistic economic argument that a finite "pie" of jobs exists in the West, and that to protect it from being cut into thinner and thinner slices, strict immigration controls must be in force to keep the world's hungry at bay. This argument is flawed from an economic perspective, since immigrants do not merely take and consume resources, but also give, acting as productive forces for expanding economies. The argument also glosses over the noneconomic factors that impel a subset of immigrants—refugees—to flee their countries and seek asylum in the West.

The 1980s have seen an increased incidence of the noneconomic factors that create refugees in the third world: wars, civil strife, and persecution. New communication and transportation technologies, which had not previously been available to these underdeveloped regions, have had a dramatic effect on refugee movements and on the destination of third world refugees seeking security and freedom. Many refugees are no longer content merely to sit passively and wait in camps. For the first time significant numbers have begun to travel spontaneously, to secure their safety far from the scene of conflict and misery.

Bypassing established channels for "processing" limited numbers of refugees from overseas, those who arrive haphazardly often have entered or stayed without permission or proper documentation. Some have survived on the margins of western societies as illegal aliens; others may have applied for asylum. Before 1975 the United States received about 200 asylum applications per year; in 1985 the number had grown to more than 16,000. West Germany saw a jump from less than 9,494 applications in 1975 to 107,818 in 1980.

These increases have triggered negative reactions and led to growing restrictiveness toward asylum seekers among many western nations. But it is not a numbers game alone. Such quantitative increases are manageable for most western economies that have withstood, and even benefited from, major European refugee movements of the past. The "refugee influx" or "flood" of the 1980s has become perceived as a "burden" because of a qualitative change as well. The typical refugee profile is no longer exclusively that of a white European fleeing communism; in most cases the color has changed to black, golden, or brown; the geographical origin has moved from north to south; and the reasons for flight are no longer reducible to escape from communism. Escape from violence or deprivation and persecution from the left or right characterizes today's forced migrations.

The United States, Canada, and West European governments portray themselves as being receptive to "genuine refugees," while denying entry to "queue jumpers" and "illegal aliens." But which refugees they deem "genuine" frequently has less to do with the human rights conditions the refugee has fled, than with the extent to which the refugee resembles the Cold War refugee profile. Western refugee determinations are also often influenced by immigration admissions standards, most notably whether their admission will unite separated relatives. For example, the United States doubled its refugee admissions ceiling for Eastern Europe and the Soviet Union in 1988 to 30,000 in order to accommodate Armenians seeking to leave the U.S.S.R., most of whom were joining family members in California. Although admitted as "refugees," the Armenians were not asked by U.S. officials to articulate a fear of persecution, the basis for refugee status eligibility under the U.S. Refugee Act.

In part to discourage spontaneous refugee arrivals, the United States, Canada, and other western nations are increasingly relying on programs they have set up for the orderly processing of refugees "of special humanitarian concern" for resettlement in the West. Specific quotas are determined, and refugees wait their turn. But only a minute fraction of the world's fourteen million refugees—one percent—are even considered for resettlement.

For refugees from countries as diverse as Sri Lanka, Guatemala, Iran, Haiti, Ethiopia, Lebanon, South Africa, and El Salvador there isn't much of a market for orderly Western resettlement. The industrialized countries of the West have little to gain by offering their protection to refugees from these and other poor third world nations. They argue, often convincingly, that such refugees are better off staying nearer to home in familiar cultural surroundings where they can be integrated into local host communities with less disruption, or positioned for easier return should conditions change at home. The argument is sound only assuming that the refugees are safe and can regularize their status at some point.

Refugees seeking asylum in the West have always had a mix of economic and political motives for fleeing one life and attempting to enter a new one—the "push" of persecution, and the "pull" of opportunity. Although a small percentage of asylum applicants are purely economically motivated and file frivolous claims to shortcut the immigration system, the very existence of any economic motive in many cases has been used in the United States to veto the chance for a fair hearing of the political merits of an asylum claim.

If a refugee comes from an impoverished country such as Haiti, his claim of political persecution is likely to be dismissed. Between June 1983 and September 1987 the United States granted only 1.7 percent of Haitian asylum cases. In 1981, in the midst of the Duvalier dictatorship, the Reagan administration began a program of "interdicting" Haitian boat people before they could land. By September 1988, 16,000 Haitians had been stopped on the high seas. Only four have been granted asylum in the U.S.

Haitian refugees, fleeing a regime with a well-documented record as an abuser of human rights, should have benefited from the U.S. law that governs treatment of refugees. The Refugee Act of 1980 did away with the statute that limited U.S. concern to refugees fleeing communism or the Middle East, and in its place introduced an impartial and nonideological humanitarian standard for determining refugee status consistent with the U.N. refugee definition. But U.S. actions continue to suggest a disparity between the intent of the law and its execution.

The treatment of Central American asylum seekers shows the stance of the U.S. government to be a reaction not only against spontaneous, unauthorized entry, but to have a marked political content as well. Both Nicaragua and El Salvador have been engaged in civil wars that have led government forces to displace peasants from regions where they are suspected of aiding insurgencies. In both cases refugees have accused the military of bombing and strafing their villages and forcing them to flee. Refugee accounts often include reports of personal threats from military and paramilitary forces as well.

Despite similarities among the refugee victims of human rights abuse in Central America, the U.S. asylum approval rates for Nicaraguans—who are fleeing an unfriendly Marxist regime—are dramatically higher than for Salvadorans—who are fleeing a regime closely allied to the United States. In 1987 less than four percent of Salvadoran asylum claims were approved, while eighty-four percent of Nicaraguan claims were granted.

For all its fair intent, the Refugee Act has apparently done little to shake the pervasive bias in U.S. refugee and asylum policy. In fact refugee admissions since 1980 are as limited to people fleeing communist-dominated regimes or the Middle East as they had been before the refugee definition was changed. Before the Refugee Act went into effect refugees were not in practice individually admitted, but rather "paroled" into the country by the Attorney General in response to refugee emergencies. Of the

1,027,497 refugees paroled into the United States between the time of the 1956 Hungarian Revolt and 1979, only 2,000—less than 0.3 percent—were from noncommunist countries. After the Refugee Act went into effect, from October 1981 through May 1987, only 780 refugees—or 0.2 percent—were admitted to the United States from countries not dominated by communism or from outside the Middle East.

Although less explicitly ideological in their biases, most of the nations of Western Europe, as well as Canada, are no less restrictionist in their treatment of third world asylum seekers. Throughout the West border controls have tightened and asylum approval rates have plunged.

Switzerland in the 1980s, the home of the U.N. High Commissioner for Refugees and traditionally a haven for the persecuted, shows how far European nations have strayed from the principles of protection for asylum seekers. In April 1987 a Swiss referendum calling for more restrictive measures against asylum seekers passed by a two-to-one margin. New regulations prevent asylum requests from being made from within Switzerland. They are now held at bay at Swiss border crossings, and denied applicants are subject to detention pending deportation. Asylum approval rates in 1987 dropped to nine percent, in contrast to the modest sixteen percent approval rate in 1984.

In West Germany the number of persons even applying for asylum dropped by more than forty percent in 1987 following measures blocking access of would-be asylum seekers to the refugee determination system. A recent law calls for the rejection of asylum seekers who transit through "safe" third countries before applying for asylum in Germany.

The focus on formal documentation is an attempt to impose order on a phenomenon that by its very nature is haphazard: refugee flight. Refugees rarely have the luxury of planning their escape. They are people who fear that their own governments will persecute them. To require a person who fears mistreatment by his government to approach that same government for permission to leave flies in the face of common sense. The prevailing law-enforcement approach that treats refugees as an immigration problem is unsuited to the reality that impels many people to seek asylum in the first place. Often the refugee who flees his country without documentation is not attempting to cheat the system by jumping the queue; he simply has no other choice.

It is understandable for governments, as well as individuals, to assess social problems in terms of the effect they will have on themselves. The influx of large numbers of third world asylum seekers has undoubtedly had a disquieting impact on the western industrialized democracies. But that impact is not the only reality, nor the most compelling. Refugees do not, ultimately, represent an immigration problem. In the starkest terms they are a human rights problem, victims or potential victims of torture and other forms of deprivation and mistreatment because of their political beliefs, ethnicity, or religion. Blocking avenues of escape, whether through interdiction of boats, fining of airlines, or denial of entry at land border crossings, may solve an immigration dilemma and subtly enforce a foreign policy agenda, but at an intolerable cost in terms of the value we place on human life and liberty.

Forged visas, prepared by smugglers' equipment *(left),* are used by Iranian refugees to circumvent Swedish law. Strict visa requirements, combined with sanctions against airlines *(above),* for carrying passengers without visas, are being used increasingly by western nations to deter asylum seekers.

VISA REQUIREMENTS AND AIRLINE FINES

Strict visa requirements often make it impossible for would-be refugees to leave their countries of origin in the first place. Restrictive visa requirements are often combined with heavy sanctions on airlines for carrying passengers who do not have the requisite visa. In 1985 the United Kingdom for the first time required visas of a Commonwealth country—Sri Lanka, the country of origin for significant numbers of Tamil asylum seekers. In 1986 the U.K. also instituted visa requirements for the Indian subcontinent, Nigeria, and Ghana. A year later, the U.K. began to impose 1,000 pound fines on shipping and airline carriers that provided passage to persons lacking valid visas or passports. Similar measures have recently been enacted in Canada, the Netherlands, Switzerland, Belgium, and the Federal Republic of Germany.

BLOCKING AT BORDERS

If refugees are never admitted into a country, they may never gain access to asylum determination procedures. Aliens without valid documents are frequently turned away at border posts and airports. Belgium, which once had one of the fairest asylum systems, instituted a more restrictive policy in 1988 which transferred refugee determination from UNHCR to a government commission. Border police are now allowed to refuse entry to asylum seekers for reasons that range from a lack of proper documents to whether they have resided in one or more third countries for more than three months. Swiss border guards are also now authorized to turn away people who say they are applying for political asylum if they have come from another country of possible refuge. Those applying for asylum in Switzerland are also now required to register at designated ports of entry.

A boatload of Haitians bound for Florida is intercepted by the U.S. Coast Guard and sent back to Haiti *(below, left).* Discriminatory government actions such as interdiction provoke protest marches by fellow Haitians in the United States *(below, right).*

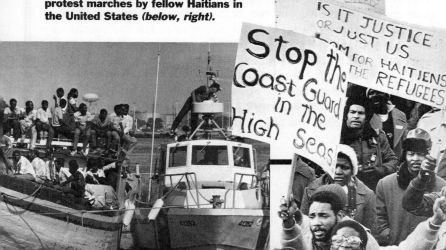

DETENTION

Since the closing of Ellis Island in 1954, aliens seeking to enter the United States, with few exceptions, were not detained. In 1980, under pressure from the Mariel Boatlift that brought 125,000 Cubans to America's shores and the simultaneous influx of undocumented Haitians, detention of "excludable aliens"—those lacking a valid passport or visa—was reintroduced in the United States. As of 1986 there were seven INS-operated detention facilities and over 1,000 non-INS facilities used to detain undocumented aliens, including state and local jails and federal prisons. In the period from October 1986 through June 1987 there were 27,670 aliens other than Mexicans detained in INS and non-INS facilities. Canada's newly enacted "deterrents and detention" law calls for detention of undocumented asylum seekers until their identities can be established, subject to review every seven days, unless the person is deemed to be a security risk.

Barbed-wire fencing at the detention facility for Salvadorans at El Centro, California *(above)* and riot gear used at the Immigration and Naturalization Service processing center in New York City *(right)* are common to detention centers in the United States.

DISTINGUISHING BETWEEN PEOPLE IN NEED

REFUGEE A person who has left his or her home country, and who has a well-founded fear of persecution upon returning to it on account of race, religion, nationality, membership in a particular social group, or political opinion.

DISPLACED PERSON An individual, who because of war or natural disaster, has been required to leave his or her home, and who may have even left his home country.

ASYLUM SEEKER A refugee who is seeking protection and shelter in a country to which he or she has fled.

MIGRANT WORKER An individual who has gone abroad to another country in order to enter into gainful employment.

POLITICAL REFUGEE A refugee who fears a threat to life or freedom on account of political belief, including deposed leaders, political opponents, etc. Also, a "refugee."

IMMIGRANT An alien who intends to establish himself or herself in a foreign country.

The U.S. Justice Department requires persons seeking asylum to fill out a form like the one above. Since 1980 only twenty-five percent of petitioners have been granted asylum.

ASYLUM DETERMINATION PROCEDURES

The process for determining whether or not asylum seekers are bona fide refugees sometimes fails to uphold asylum seekers' due process rights. These include the right to examine relevant documents and to be permitted to respond to them; to have access to legal counsel at every stage of the procedure; to have an interpreter; to communicate with the UNHCR and voluntary agencies; and to have the right of appeal. These rights are not universally observed in the West. In the United Kingdom, for example, there is no right of appeal for asylum seekers who enter without valid travel documents. A new law recently enacted in Canada will allow screening of asylum seekers for eligibility and credibility before hearing the merits of their cases. Applicants coming from "safe third countries" will be deemed ineligible and returned to those countries; applicants lacking credibility will be returned to their country of origin.

ECONOMIC REFUGEE Not technically a "refugee," but rather an individual whose sojourn is motivated by the prospect of economic betterment.

ILLEGAL ALIEN An individual who does not have permission to remain in the country in which he or she finds himself, and who may thereby face expulsion or return to the home country.

ALIEN An individual who is not recognized as a national and who cannot count on enjoyment of full legal rights in the country in which he or she is living.

DETAINEE An alien in the custody of the authorities whose case to enter or remain is being considered by those authorities.

INTERNEE An alien residing in a country who is placed in detention, often for alleged security reasons.

ILLEGAL MIGRANTS Aliens who have gone abroad, and wish to establish themselves there for personal reasons, but who have no basis on which to enter or remain in the country of sojourn.

WITHHOLDING SOCIAL BENEFITS OR EMPLOYMENT

The refugee determination procedure is often a long and drawn out process, sometimes taking years to complete. Asylum seekers waiting in European countries are frequently prohibited from employment, making them dependent on public assistance. In Germany they cannot hold paying jobs for five years and are required to live in collective housing unless they can show that they have alternative living arrangements that will not result in greater public expenditures. In 1984, when all applicants were required to stay in collective housing, they spent an average of one-to-two years in them. In Sweden, asylum-seekers are prohibited from working and are housed in "investigation centers" pending a determination of their status.

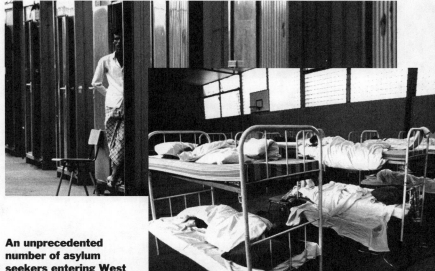

An unprecedented number of asylum seekers entering West Germany through East Berlin in 1986 created a shortage of housing for people awaiting refugee status hearings. A Sri Lankan spends his days in a construction container provided by the government *(above)*. Cramped rows of bunk beds, set up in a school auditorium, provide additional shelter *(above, right)*.

DEPORTATION

Article 33 of the United Nations Convention Relating to the Status of Refugees prohibits the return of a refugee to the frontiers of territories where his life or freedom would be threatened. Western nations, however, have been increasingly willing to return asylum seekers to "safe third countries" through which they passed before arriving in the West. This leaves open the question of what constitutes a "safe third country." Turkey, for instance, does not regard Iranians as refugees and assumes they will move on and seek permanent asylum elsewhere. When Iranian asylum seekers were rejected in Europe or North America and deported to Turkey, Turkey reserved the right to return them to Iran. More than six hundred were forcibly returned in 1987, at least fourteen of whom were recognized refugees under the UNHCR mandate. Many have reportedly been returned by Turkish border police in the remote frontier regions.

Increasingly, asylum seekers in Europe and the United States are threatened with deportation to their homelands or to a third country. Denied asylum in Germany, a Pakistani refugee is escorted under guard to a special plane that will take him back to Karachi.

A basic measure of a civilized society is the way it treats strangers. Where migration is forced for political reasons, whether it be mass persecution or individual exile, the stranger is a refugee. While refugees have been with us for a long time, at least since the era of the Nation-State itself, the needs of today's refugees for legal protection are unprecedented.

Vast numbers of refugees have been forced out and deprived of the protection of their homelands. The United Nations High Commissioner for Refugees now counts some fourteen million asylum seekers fleeing from insurgent activities or counterinsurgent strategies. Though not political opponents, they are displaced and threatened because governments or guerrillas suspect them, and hope to gain tactical advantage by driving them from their homes. Most modern refugees are innocent civilians who have the misfortune to live in areas of conflict.

The reception given to refuges in countries of asylum varies, with authorities sometimes reacting with compassion to the influx, but more often reacting with callousness. With increasing frequency, refugees are rejected at a border or shore, left to perish at sea, placed in detention upon arrival, or deprived of the opportunity for employment, education, or family life. These policies of abuse are designed to mistreat asylum seekers, encouraging them to leave and go elsewhere, or, more to the point, not to seek refuge in the first place. Euphemistically called "humane deterrence" measures, these policies are fundamentally anti-humanitarian.

Prospects for a solution of refugee situations are always uncertain. As long as the causes of flight remain, refugees resist returning home. Resettlement in third countries is available to less than one percent of the fourteen million. Even integration into the local population is denied many asylum seekers. They are literally persons without homelands.

Legal protection is just as much a patchwork for refugees. The government of the country of origin cannot or will not provide protection. International refugee law protects from return only those who fear individualized persecution for certain specified reasons. While the right to leave one's country is recognized under the law, no State is correspondingly obliged to grant asylum to any refugee. Humanitarian law protects noncombatant civilians in times of war and civil strife. Human rights law is universal, but, more often than not, aspirational and not binding on States. Protection for persons forced out of their homelands and in need of refuge is thus largely a matter of discretion and governmental grace. Such basic needs, however, deserve to be the subject of legal imperative. Refuge is a fundamental human right. Given the dimension of the problem, the international community must act to address these needs. If a new law be deemed necessary, we offer the following proposed Covenant on the Rights of Refugees.   ARTHUR HELTON

CHANCE FOR CHANGE: A COVENANT ON THE RIGHTS OF PEOPLE IN NEED OF REFUGE

1 All nations must recognize the inherent dignity and equal rights of all members of the human family, and ensure that they are observed in times of need.

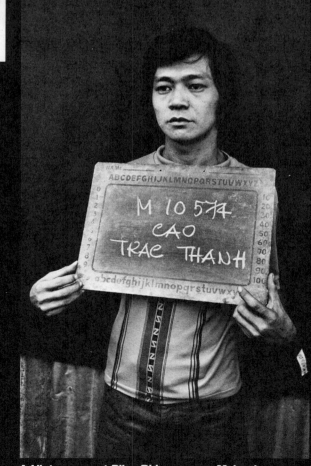

A Vietnamese at Pilau Bidong camp, Malaysia, is photographed with his name and boat number.

2 Everyone has the right to life, liberty, and security, and every nation has the responsibility to enforce these rights.

3 Everyone has the right to a homeland and, if under the jurisdiction of a State, the right to citizenship. No person shall be arbitrarily deprived of a homeland.

A Palestinian in Naplouse, West Bank, hurls stones at an Israeli Army helicopter.

4 No civilian shall be displaced because of military conflict, except for his own protection.

Tibetan monks in exile in India lead a protest march against the Chinese repression in Tibet.

5 Everyone shall be equal before the law, and entitled to due process of law. Among those in need of refuge, there shall be no distinctions, exclusions, restrictions, or preferences based on race, gender, national or ethnic origin, religion, social status, or political opinion.

Russian refusenik, Eugeni Lein, denied an exit visa by Soviet authorities, stands trial in Moscow.

An "illegal" alien testifies before a U.S. Congressional hearing in New York City.

6 **When people have been forced out of a homeland, they shall have a right to asylum where they flee. Asylum is not to be considered an unfriendly act toward the nation from which refugees have fled.**

7 Every person has the right to seek asylum without interference, including the right not to be turned back at borders or otherwise impeded in the asylum process.

8 Everyone who exercises the right of asylum shall be treated with dignity, and the essentials of life shall be guaranteed, including freedom of movement, travel documents, education, employment, and family reunification.

A Cambodian woman, with medical instructions marked on her forehead, rests in Sa Keo camp, Thailand.

Haitian women wait at Camp Krome detention center, Florida.

9 Abusive detention is incompatible with an asylum seeker's right to dignified treatment.

10 Children shall, in all circumstances, be among the first to receive protection and assistance.

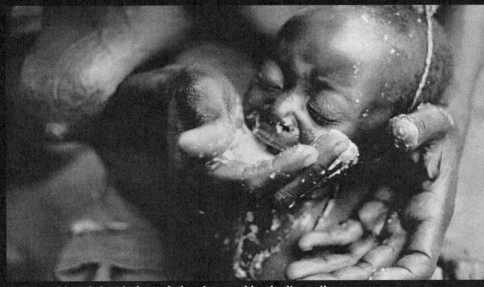

A Mozambican infant is force-fed maize porridge by its mother.

11 When an individual has been deprived of a homeland, and voluntary return is prevented, provision shall be made for a durable immigration status with rights and privileges equal to those of nationals, whether in the form of permanent refuge in the country of asylum or by resettlement elsewhere.

Demonstrators in a Paris suburb march in support of equal rights.

12 **It is the responsibility of nations to share the burden of providing refuge, taking into account differences in wealth and resources among nations.**

Famine victim, Ethiopia, 1983

THE SOUND OF SILENCE

CAROLE KISMARIC

This account of the world's refugees attempts to penetrate a silence that in recent years has deepened around the world. While fragments of the refugees' story emerge occasionally in dismal, grainy newspaper pictures and in flickering television images that dramatize the daily life of millions of people—one of relentless oppression, unimaginable terror, and the brutal denial of the rights we take for granted—the refugee remains wedged on the rim of our consciousness, a symbol of vulnerability in a world that lacks meaningful symbols. His story is a shocking reminder of how in the twentieth century we have come to disregard the individual.

These fourteen million men, women, and children are obscured, concealed behind the dust suspended in airless refugee camps—located in time and space, but always far, far away. We, on the other hand, are caught in a different kind of limbo. Bound culturally, socially, psychologically, and spiritually to our culture, we cannot reconcile our lives with the injustice and poverty that characterize a world so radically different from our own. We cannot identify with the modern refugee, and we are reluctant to imagine his fate as ours. So silence fills the void between us, and any messages we receive are noted, then deflected.

The message of *Forced Out* aims straight at the heart: that every single one of the thousands of human creatures trudging across deserts and over mountain passes, through valleys and along shorelines, over gulfs of water and grassy plains has a name and a history. Farmers, shepherds, clerks, shopkeepers, doctors, teachers, traders, leaders, followers, mothers, fathers, children—each has survived countless betrayals and is a person among people.

Most of the people alive today live in the third world. They have been bruised by shaky economies and political upheavals, as they ride out the stormy transitions from supremacy to subjugation to self-determination. They have thrived on their own terms, with rich traditions that have made significant contributions to the quality of the world's experience. The dynamic that has shaken these people loose is complicated. It is enough to note here that after centuries of distancing ourselves from the third world, the industrialized countries can no longer ignore or dismiss the vigor of their culture.

At the end of World War II, there were ten million displaced people—innocent victims of a barbarous war. Within a decade, they had been resettled—either returned home or generally set on their ways—largely as a result of the concern, determination, and generosity of a world community that sought to make the impracticable possible.

It was a time when the individual was respected—even revered. Justice, for the most part, mediated the interests of the whole; and the world, recovering from the nightmare of war, recommitted itself to recognizing barbarism, to monitoring the cruel self-interest of power, and to stopping the forces that could wipe out the individual. We felt the deep injustice that made the individual, swept up by the flow of events, the victim of history. We recognized then that human sacrifice was shocking and painfully horrific, and we insisted that genocide would never again be repeated.

By 1989 fourteen million individuals had been pushed out of their homelands by indiscriminate violence and purposeful persecution. Uprooted, pouring across breachable borders, no one knows for certain how many they are. Their lives have been torn apart, crushed. One journalist has described the modern refugee as "an actor who has fallen off the stage." If one assumes that by fleeing the refugee gives up his or her responsibility in the battle for justice and equality, one grasps a small part of the story. It is important to understand that refugees are pawns in a world shaped by superpowers; their experience is determined by political motives and not personal or humanitarian ones. Little of what happens to them is of their choosing.

In the forty-four years that have passed since World War II ended, our hearts have closed down; our intellect has snapped into place; and our response to the problems of the refugee is an unthinking cynicism. We are too small: "it" is too big. We have turned off the voice of protest and traded in any memory that could stir up the pain of the past, for a silence and indifference that shields us from the perilous future. As we peer into the twenty-first century and the civilization we will claim, we are no longer willing to exercise our imagination, to project what humanity might achieve—to believe that fourteen million people can be assisted in returning home.

Maybe because these refugees are not, for the most part, our European ancestors; maybe because we sense the powerful cultural changes they bring with them; maybe because we have ruled too long and cannot accept that they want to take their dignified place alongside us, we seem to have easily, and with very little guilt, put to one side the fact that protecting their rights is our responsibility.

Forced Out allows the refugee to tell his own story in a voice that is authoritative. It is a story that is senseless, savage, and tragic. But in reality, this account only skims the surface of the refugees' experience. To wrench more truth from their story, to come closer to the terror and humiliation each must endure, *Forced Out* would have to bleed with every turn of the page, cry out when you skip a word, and scream when you close its covers. The silence would then begin to be filled.

With the help of Honduran soldiers, Miskito Indians from Mocoron camp clamber down the banks of the Rio Coco River to boats that will take them home to Nicaragua.

ACKNOWLEDGMENTS

There were many individuals and organizations whose generosity knew no limits in helping us gather the photographs and the facts that would best tell the refugees' story. Unstinting with their time, ideas, and support, they helped make this book possible, and we are very grateful; each is truly a contributor. We thank first those individuals who helped us shape the ideas and determine the facts.

At the U.S. Committee for Refugees, Roger Winter, the director, inspired creative thinking. Virginia Hamilton continually provided information essential to the story. Bill Frelick, Court Robinson, and Tom Brennan also offered invaluable assistance.

Roy Williams and Susan Stark of the International Rescue Committee spent many hours reviewing our ideas and leading us to new sources at critical points in the project. At Cultural Survival, Jason Clay helped us understand the importance of homeland to people and to the book. Anne Manuel of Americas Watch was diligent in researching the facts about Central America. Phillip Rudge of the European Consultation on Refugees and Exiles in London was sensitive, and his compassion was an inspiration.

At the United Nations High Commissioner for Refugees, Guilherme Da-Chuna, Judith Kumin, and Patricia Weiss-Fagen were especially helpful. John Miles, United Nations Works and Relief Agency; Masoor Suhail, Pakistan Mission to the United Nations; Peter Rose, Smith College; Dr. B. E. Harrell-Bond, Director, Refugee Studies Program, Oxford University; Mary Ann Siegfried, editor, "Afghanistan Forum"; and Diane Nelson, Joel Morelos, Walter Stockli, Rudolf Klever, Dr. Glenn Randall, and James Appe understood the importance of the publication and made valuable resources available to us. Without the assistance of America's Watch consultant Joe Eldridge and Patrick Ahern of the Catholic Relief Services, our trip to the refugee camps in Honduras, which made our subject real to us, would not have been feasible. Joli Stahl led us to them, and Jim Solkin and Dominique Doutrelign were our guides.

Our picture research began at "The New York Times," and Bob Medina, who grasped the project immediately, and his staff deserve special recognition. Without their patience and willingness, the picture research on this project would not have been possible. Many photographers have generously offered their ideas, picture files, and time. But without the support of Derrill Bazzy, Ed Grazda, David Heiden, and Gilles Peress, our job would have been joyless. Our friends in Europe contributed significantly to finding the impossible pictures. We are particularly indebted to Christiane Breustedt, Dag Alveng, Brenda Marsh, and Torgny Warn.

Many of the photographers and pictures agencies have relaxed rules, made exceptions, and creatively stretched to help us realize Forced Out. Jocelyn Benzecant of JB Pictures offered valuable advice that improved the book. Nat Andriani of Wide World never gave up on our numerous requests, and Elisabeth Gallin of Magnum was always there. Robert Pledge, director of Contact Press Images; Woody Camp and Midge Keator of Woodfin Camp & Associates; and Jim Carlson of the "Christian Science Monitor" gave us access at critical times. Frederique d'Angeljean of Sygma, Paris; Eliane Laffont of the New York Sygma office; Denise Close of SIPA, Paris; and Jennifer Coley of Gamma-Liaison met our wide-ranging requests for pictures with determination. Doris O'Neill, Beth Zarcone, and Debra Cohen of Time, Inc. were particularly understanding. Jay Nubile, who made numerous prints for the book, worked conscientiously, maintaining his high standards.

The Institute for Contemporary Art, P.S. 1 Museum in Long Island City, provided a studio in which the book was created, and Lisa Semple of ABC also provided space in which to work.

Our sincere gratitude extends to the following individuals who made this book better than we could have achieved alone: at the Human Rights Watch Committee, Juan Mendez, Linda Long, Sophie Silberberg, and Betsy Fee. At the Lawyers Committee, Mitchell Hartman; at the UNHCR, Terry Kratovil, Serge Malé, Anne-Lisa Hollman; at the Refugee Studies Program, Oxford University, Helen Wooldridge and Johan Cels; at Amnesty International in Paris, Patrick Delouvin; at Médecins Sans Frontières, François Jean; at El Rescate, Sarah Stephens; at UNRWA, Valerie Walker; at Magnum, Neil Burgess in London, Patricia Strathern in Paris, and Susan Duca and Bob Danin in New York; at Archive, Ann Schneider; at Black Star, Howard Chapnick; at Sygma, New York, Dallas Chang; at Gamma-Liaison, New York, Daniel Sorine; at VU in Paris, Christian Caujolle; and at Wheeler Pictures, Paul Wheeler.

The following individuals helped in various ways, and we thank them: Ron Arias, Elisabeth Biondi, Norbert Schady, Dr. Jonathan Fine, Margaret McKelvy, Dan Connell, Robert Kirschenbaum, Dr. F. Allodi, Joan Simalchik, Kerry Connor, Beatriz Manz, Jennifer Schirmer, Martin Diskin, Joel Charny, Paula Woorby, Mike Scott, Hiram Ruiz, Ann Ewing, Susan Forbes-Martin, Barry Stein, Barney Rubin, Mel Lehman, Michael McConnell, Richard Grimmett, Nancy Lorrence, Stephen Kass, Anne Rogin, Ulyssess Santa Maria, Henri and Bora Stern, Jean Charles Blanc, Gatan Mooto, Robert Stevens, Yseult Freilicher, Amy Roberts, Sarah Lazin, Victor Kovner, Mary Shanahan, and Susan Kismaric.

We thank all the photographers in the book, and especially: Jerry Berndt, Hervé Gloaguen, Mike Goldwater, Michel Setboun, Alain Keler, Chris Steele Perkins, and John Isaac. Eve Arnold, the distinguished photographer, was a catalyst in bringing The J. M. Kaplan Fund and Carole Kismaric together.

Forced Out exists because of Joan Davidson. A book about refugees was her idea, and it is her determination, commitment, and creative support that inspire every page.

ABOUT THE CONTRIBUTORS

MARK MALLOCH BROWN is in charge of international political campaigns for the Sawyer Miller Group. He has worked on the presidential campaign of President Corazon Aquino, as well as on campaigns and government programs in Latin America, the United States, and Europe. Formerly a political journalist for "The Economist," he started the "Economist Development Report," a newsletter on development and refugee issues. He worked for the United Nations High Commissioner for Refugees running the field program for Cambodian refugees in Thailand and serving as deputy chief of its Emergency Unit.

BILL FRELICK is a policy analyst specializing in asylum issues in the United States, the Middle East, and South Asia, with the U.S. Committee for Refugees in Washington, D.C. He has been with the USCR since 1984 where his responsibilities include writing and researching for "Refugee Reports" and "The World Refugee Survey." A longtime human rights activist, he is a former board member of Amnesty International U.S.A.

ARTHUR HELTON is director of the Political Asylum Project of the Lawyers Committee for Human Rights and chair of the Advisory Committee to the New York State Inter-Agency Task Force on Immigration Affairs. He has authored numerous articles, testified in Congress and Federal Court, and litigated in several cases concerning immigration and refugee issues.

JERI LABER is executive director of Helsinki Watch and is active in Americas Watch and in Asia Watch. She was executive director of the International Freedom to Publish Committee of the Association of American Publishers. Her interest in Soviet affairs and, in particular, in the Soviet dissident movement, led to her activities in the field of human rights.

CAROLE KISMARIC is a writer, editor, and producer of books. As editorial director of Aperture, she edited more than forty books in the Aperture program including Diane Arbus: Magazine Work, Telex: Iran, and Lisette Model. She originated over ten books in the Time-Life Photography Series including Documentary Photography and the Art of Photography. Currently she is working with Marvin Heiferman on a series of books to be distributed by Vintage Books in the fall of 1989.

ARYEH NEIER is executive director of Human Rights Watch, vice-chairman of the Fund for Free Expression, and adjunct professor of law at New York University. He has contributed to more than twenty books and three-hundred articles on the subject of law and human rights.

WILLIAM SHAWCROSS won the 1980 George Polk Book Award and the 1979 Sidney Hillman Foundation Prize Award for Sideshow: Kissinger, Nixon, and the Destruction of Cambodia. His sequel Quality of Mercy, published in 1984 by Simon and Schuster, received the Freedom From Hunger Medal Award. His latest book, The Shah's Last Ride, is an account of the shah of Iran's exile and death.

HUMAN RIGHTS WATCH and its regional committees—Africa Watch, Americas Watch, Asia Watch, Helsinki Watch, and Middle East Watch—monitor and promote human rights worldwide. Human Rights Watch devotes special attention to protecting human rights in the context of political and military conflicts that force people to flee their homes and countries; to protecting citizens persecuted for monitoring their own governments' human rights practices; to influencing the foreign policy of the United States to protect human rights; and to publishing reliable, comprehensive, and timely reports on human rights conditions in countries of varying political character and geopolitical alignment.

THE J. M. KAPLAN FUND is a private family foundation based in New York. It supports local environmental and historic conservation, rational land-use planning, the arts, civil liberties, and the international cause of human rights.

FURTHER READING

GENERAL

Refugees: A Problem of Our Time. Louise W. Holborn. Scarecrow Press, Metuchen, New Jersey, 1975.

Refugees: Dynamics of Displacement. A report for the Independent Commission on International Humanitarian Issues. Zed Books, Ltd, London and Atlantic Highlands, New Jersey, 1986.

Refugee: The Vietnam Experience. Edited by Lesleyanne Hawthorne. Oxford University Press, Melbourne, 1982.

The Spirit of Survival. Gail Sheehy. William Morrow and Co., New York, 1986.

The Unwanted: European Refugees in the Twentieth Century. Michael R. Marrus. Oxford University Press, Melbourne, 1985.

World Refugee Survey, 1988. U.S. Committee for Refugees, Washington, D.C.

PART I: FORCED TO FLEE

Afghanistan: The Soviet War. Edward Girardet. St. Martins Press, New York, 1987.

Another Day of Life. Ryszard Kapuscinski. Translated by William R. Brand and Kataryna Mroczkowska-Brand. Wolff/Harcourt Brace Jovanovich, San Diego, 1987.

Blood of the Innocent: Victims of the Contras' War in Nicaragua. Teofilo Cabestrero. Translated by Robert R. Barr. Orbis Books, Maryknoll, New York, 1985.

Cry of the People: The Struggle for Human Rights in Latin America: The Catholic Church in Conflict with U.S. Policy. Penny Lernoux. Penguin Books, New York, 1980.

Cuzcatlan: Where the Southern Sea Beats. Manlio Argueta. Translated by Clark Hansen. Vintage Books, New York, 1987.

Days and Nights of Love and War. Eduardo Galeano. Monthly Review Press, New York, 1983.

Destroying Ethnic Identity. The Kurds of Turkey. Helsinki Watch, New York, 1988.

El Salvador: Work of Thirty Photographers. Text by Carolyn Forché. Edited by Harry Mattison, Susan Meiselas, and Fae Rubinstein. Writers and Readers, New York and London, 1983.

Guatemala: Eternal Spring, Eternal Tyranny. Jean-Marie Simon. W.W. Norton, New York, 1988.

Guatemala: Tyranny on Trial. Testimony of the Permanent People's Tribunal. Edited by Susanne Jonas, Ed McCaughan, and Elizabeth Sutherland Martinez. Synthesis Publications, San Francisco, 1984.

Introduction to The CIA's Nicaragua Manual. Joanne Omang. Vintage Books, New York, 1985.

I, Rigoberta Menchú: An Indian Woman in Guatemala. Rigoberta Menchú. Edited by Elisabeth Burgos-Debray. Verso Publishers, London, 1984.

Move Your Shadow: South Africa, Black and White. Joseph Lelyveld. Penguin Books, New York, 1985.

Nightmare Revisited: Human Rights in El Salvador 1987—88. Americas Watch, New York, 1988.

Nunca Mas: The Report of the Argentine National Commission of the Disappeared. Farrar, Straus & Giroux, in association with Index on Censorship, New York.

Prison Diaries. Eduard Kuznetov. Scarborough Books, Stein & Day, Briarcliff Manor, New York, 1975.

The Question of Palestine. Edward W. Said. Vintage Books, New York, 1979.

Refugees of a Hidden War. Beatrice Manz. State University of New York, Albany, 1988.

Refusnik: Trapped in the Soviet Union. Mark Ya Azbel. Paragon House, New York, 1987.

The Persecution of Human Rights Monitors. 1987—88: A Worldwide Survey. Human Rights Watch, 1988.

Valiant Women in War and Exile. Sally Hayton-Keeva. City Lights, San Francisco, 1987.

PART II: HAVEN OR PRISON?

After the Last Sky: Palestinian Lives. Edward W. Said. Pantheon Books, New York, 1986.

The Boat People. Bruce Grant. Penguin Books, New York, 1979.

The Brutality of Nations. Dan Jacobs. Alfred A. Knopf. New York, 1987.

Famine, A Man-Made Disaster? Independent Commission on International Humanitarian Issues. Vintage Books, New York, 1985.

Fighting the Famine. Nigel Twose. Photographs by Mike Goldwater. Pluto Press, London, 1985.

Forced to Move: Salvadoran Refugees in Honduras. Renato Camarda. Solidarity Publications, San Francisco, 1985.

Imposing Aid: Emergency Assistance to Refugees. B. E. Harrell-Bond. Oxford University Press, Oxford and New York, 1986.

Just Waiting to Die? Cambodian Refugees in Thailand. Tony Jackson. Oxfam, England.

Stateless in Gaza. Paul Colassi and Clive Robson. Zed Books, London and Atlantic Highlands, New Jersey, 1986.

The Quality of Mercy: Cambodia, Holocaust and Modern Conscience. William Shawcross. Simon & Schuster, New York, 1984.

Refugees from Vietnam in Hong Kong. Refugee Action. Oakwood, Derby, England, 1986.

Rice, Rivalry, and Politics: Managing Cambodian Relief. Linda Mason and Roger Brown. University of Notre Dame Press, Notre Dame, Indiana, 1983.

Shallow Graves: Two Women and Vietnam. Wendy Wilder Larsen and Tran Thi Nga. Random House, New York, 1986.

Socio-Economic Evaluation of the Khmer Camps on the Thai/Kampuchean Border. Dr. Josephine Reynell. Refugee Studies Program, Queen Elizabeth House, Oxford, England.

PART II: SHUTTING THE DOORS

A Seventh Man: Migrant Workers in Europe. John Berger. Photographs by Jean Mohr. Viking Press, New York, 1975.

Asylum in Europe: A Handbook for Agencies Assisting Refugees. European Consultation on Refugees and Exiles, London, 1983.

Calculated Kindness: Refugees and America's Half-Open Door 1945—Present. Gilbert Loescher and John A. Scanlan. The Free Press, New York, 1986.

Restrictive Asylum Policy in Europe. A Report of the Seminar Held in Zeist, The Netherlands, January 16—18, 1985. European Consultation on Refugees and Exiles, London, 1985.

Sanctuary: The New Underground Railroad. Kenny Golden and Michael McConnell. Orbis Books, Maryknoll, New York, 1986.

The Stranger Within Your Gates: Uprooted People in the World Today. André Jacques. World Council of Churches, Geneva, 1985.

OTHER SOURCES

The Lawyers Committee for Human Rights is a public interest law center that promotes compliance with internationally recognized human rights law and legal principles. 330 Seventh Avenue, New York, New York 10001. Publications of special interest:

From the Ashes: Justice in El Salvador. 1987.

Haiti: Rights Denied. 1985.

Mother of Exiles: Imprisoned in America. (with Helsinki Watch) 1986.

The Reagan Administration's Record on Human Rights in 1988 (with Human Rights Watch).

Seeking Shelter: Cambodians in Thailand. 1987.

Cultural Survival supports projects designed to help indigenous peoples survive, both physically and culturally. They publish "Cultural Survival Quarterly." 11 Divinity Avenue, Cambridge, Massachusetts 02138. Publications of special interest:

"Death and Disorder in Guatemala," vol. 7:1, 1983.

"Land Rights: Strategies for Survival," vol. 10:2, 1986.

"Militarization and Indigenous Peoples. Part I. Americas and the Pacific," vol. 11:3, 1987; Part II. "Africa, Asia, and the Middle East," vol. 11:4, 1987.

"Politics and the Ethiopian Famine 1984—85," Jason W. Clay and Bonnie K. Holcomb. Occasional paper, no. 20. February 1986.

"The Search for Work," vol. 7:4, 1983.

U.S. Committee for Refugees is a public information and advocacy program of the American Council for Nationalities Service that encourages the American public to participate actively in efforts to assist the world's refugees. It publishes an annual World Refugee Survey and "Issue Papers," studies of important refugee concerns. 1025 Vermont Avenue NW, Suite 920, Washington, DC 20005. Publications of special interest:

Beyond the Headlines: Refugees in the Horn of Africa. January 1988.

Cambodians in Thailand: People on the Edge. December 1985.

Despite a Generous Spirit: Denying Asylum in the United States. December 1986.

Refugees from Mozambique: Shattered Land, Fragile Asylum. November, 1986.

Uprooted Angolans: From Crisis to Catastrophe. August 1987.

The Refugee Studies Program is an international archive and study center for issues pertaining to refugees worldwide. It undertakes and supports research on matters ranging from the daily lives of refugees to their protection under international law. University of Oxford, Queen Elizabeth House, 21 St. Giles, Oxford OX1 3LA, England.

CREDITS

PICTURE SOURCES

Cover: David Heiden. Inside front cover: Sebastiao Salgado, Magnum Photos. Back inside cover: Derrill Bazzy. Pages 2, 3: Michel Setboun, Rapho. 4: Dennis Gordon. 5: John Tlumacki, "The Boston Globe." 6, 7: Athens News Agency, Athens. 8, 9: Wide World. 10: Bill Reinke, "The Miami News." 11: David Parker, Alpha. 12, 13: UPI/Bettmann. 14, 15: Sebastiao Salgado, Magnum. 16, 17: Judah Passow, JB Pictures. 18, 19: Wide World. 20: Jorma Puusa, Photoreporters/Lehtikuva. 21: Sabetta, UPI/Bettmann. 22: Robin Moyer, Black Star. 23—26: Bill Burke, Archive Pictures. 32, 33: Arturo Robles, JB Pictures. 34: François Sully, Black Star. 35: Derrill Bazzy. 37: top, Jeff Harmon; bottom, Robert Caputo. 38: Jean Mohr. 40, 41: Susan Meiselas, Magnum. 42, 43: Kenneth Silverman, Wheeler Pictures. 44, 45: James Nachtwey, Magnum. 46, 47: left, John Hoagland, Gamma-Liaison; right, Alon Reininger, Contact Press Images. 48: left, top to bottom: Patrick Chauvel, Sygma; Derrill Bazzy; Susan Meiselas, Magnum; Arturo Robles, Black Star; right, top to bottom: Miguel Solis, Reuters; Richard Cross; Susan Meiselas, Magnum. 49: left, top to bottom: James Nachtwey, Magnum; Mike Goldwater, Network; Etienne Montes, Gamma-Liaison; Susan Meiselas, Magnum; right, top to bottom: John Hoagland, Gamma-Liaison; Mike Goldwater, Network; Derrill Bazzy; Alon Reininger, Contact. 50, 51: Jerry Berndt. 52: Physicians for Human Rights. 52, 53: Jean-Marie Simon, Visions. 54, 55: Enrique Shore, Woodfin Camp & Associates. 57: Orbis Books. 58—59: Gilles Peress, Magnum. 60—61: Kenneth Silverman, Wheeler Pictures. 62, 63: Pat Goudvis. 64: Michael Miller. 66: Wide World. 67: Wide World except top, left: Howard Sochurek, *Life* magazine (c) Time, Inc. 68: left, top to bottom: Larry Price; Wide World; James Nachtwey, Magnum; Raghu Rai, Magnum; Suzanne Green, UPI/Bettmann; right, top to bottom: UPI/Bettmann; UPI/Bettmann; Thomas Hartwell, *Time*; William Campbell, *Time*; Wide World. 70: right, top to bottom: "The New York Times"; Reuters; Reuters. 71: left, top to bottom: Agence France Presse; Harper & Row; UPI/Bettmann; right, top to bottom: Andrew Sacks; "The New York Times"; UPI/Bettmann; Sygma. 72: Michael Miller. 74, 75: Alain Keler, Sygma. 76: Bill Burke, Archive. 77: Jose More, UPI/Bettmann. 78: Barry Shlachter, Wide World. 80: Eddie Adams. 81: Andrew Holbrooke. 83: Committee for a Free Afghanistan. 84: "The New York Times." 87: Gilles Peress, Magnum. 88: Mansanori Kobayashi. 89: Hervé Gloaguen, Rapho. 90—92: Gilles Peress, Magnum. 94, 95: Gilles Peress, Magnum. 96, 97: Ed Grazda. 96: bottom, Michel Philippot, Sygma. 97: bottom, Laurent Maous, Gamma-Liaison. 98, 99: Burk Uzzle, Archive. 100: left, top to bottom: Gilles Peress, Magnum; Paul Fusco, Magnum; United Nations Relief and Works Agency; Rudi Meisel, Visum; right, top to bottom: Gilles Peress, Magnum; Roland Neveu, Gamma-Liaison; Mike Abrahams, Network; Jan Goodwin. 101: Mansanori Kobayshi. 102, 103: John Isacc, United Nations. 104, 105. Gilles Peress, Magnum. 106, 107: David Heiden. 108, 109: background, Tom Haley, Sipa Press. 108: top to bottom, R. Burrows, UNHCR; Ed Grazda; David Burnett, Contact; Martha Ryan; Gilles Peress, Magnum. 109: top to bottom: M. Vanappelghem, UNHCR; J. M. Micaud, UNHCR; Hervé Gloaguen, UNHCR; Ed Grazda; John Vink, Agence VU; Alain Keler, Sygma. 110, 111: Mansanori Kobayashi. 111: Sharon J. Wohlmuth, "The Philadelphia Inquirer." 112: top to bottom, Larry P. Goodson; Kenneth Silverman, Wheeler Pictures; Jean Gaumy, Magnum. 113: Reen Pilkington. 114, 115: David Heiden. 116: Collection of Neil Boothby; 119: left, Sebastiao Salgado, Magnum; right, Terry Fincher, Photographers International; James Nachtwey, Magnum. 120: left, top to bottom: UPI/Bettmann; Mike Goldwater, Network; Alain Keler, Sygma; Eve Arnold, Magnum; right, top to bottom: Kip Warr, Oxfam America; David Heiden; Anthony Suau, Black Star. 122: Joe Lawton. 124, 125: background, UPI/Bettmann, courtesy CBS News. 125: Derrill Bazzy. 126: D. A. Bertoni, UNHCR. 128, 129: background, James Nachtwey, Magnum. 129: United Nations. 130: Hervé Gloaguen, Rapho. 132, 133: background, Christine Spengler, Sygma. 133: Bill Burke, Archive. 134: UNRWA. 136, 137: background, James Nachtwey, Magnum. 137: Bruno Barbey, Magnum. 138: David Hurn, Magnum. 139: top to bottom, Mohamed Lounes, Gamma-Liaison; UPI/Bettmann; Steve Wall. 140: top to bottom, Mohamed Lounes, Gamma-Liaison; Don Wright, "The Miami News"; David Hoffman, Camera Press Ltd. 141: left, top to bottom: Leonard Freed, Magnum; Olle Lindstedt, Mira Agency; Henning Christoph; right, top to bottom: Leonard Freed, Magnum; Rune Lislerud, Samfoto; David Hoffman, Camera Press. 142: Peter Marlow, Sygma. 144, 145: Bruno Kellenberger, Ringier Dokumentationszentrum. 146, 147: Holger Kulick. 148: G. Liu, UPI/Bettmann. 148, 149: Wide World. 150, 151: top, Jeff Wasserman, "The Globe and Mail," Toronto; bottom, Leif Engberg, Photoreporters/Pressens Bild. 152, 153: Gary Monroe. 154—156: Elke Bruhn-Hoffmann, Wide World. 157: Metin Yilmaz. 158, 159: Art Walker, "The Chicago Tribune." 160, 161: Jean- Louis Atlan, Sygma. 162: UNHCR. 166: left, top to bottom: Lennart Isaksson, Photoreporters/Pressens Bild; Lufthansa; "News/Sun Sentinel"; Scott Stewart, Wide World; right, top to bottom: Leo Hetzel, Photoreporters; Ben Fernandez. 167: left, Lawyers Committee for Human rights; right, top to bottom: Henning Christoph; Henning Christoph; Peter Ronholz. 170: David Burnett, Contact. 172: Javier Bauluz, Reuters. 173: Sondeep Shankar, Wide World. 174: "The New York Times." 175: Jack Manning, "The New York Times." 177: David Burnett, Contact. 178: Michael Carlebach. 179: Joe Alexander, UPI/Bettmann. 181: Alain Bizos, Agence VU. 182: Chris Cartter, Grassroots International. 184: M. Bartow, UNHCR. 186: Candace Freeland. 188, 189: Gilles Peress, Magnum.

TEXT SOURCES

Pages 34, 82, 98, and 130: *Refugee: The Vietnamese Experience*, Lesleyanne Hawthorne, Oxford University Press, Melbourne, 1982; 35, 44, 46: *I, Rigoberta Menchú: An Indian Woman in Guatemala*, edited by Elisabeth Burgos-Debray (translator, Ann Wright), Verso Publishers, London, 1984; 36: "Jihad: The Fight for Afghanistan," directed by Jeff P. Harmon; 37: *Flight and Other Stories*, James Appe, Akira Press, Ltd., London, 1987; 38: "The Day Ibrahim Al-Agra Was Killed," "Index on Censorship," London, October 1986; 43: testimony to legal aid office, Archdiocese, San Salvador, 1984; 44 and 50: *Cuzcatlan: Where the Southern Sea Beats*, Manlio Argueta (translator, Clark Hansen), Vintage Books, New York, 1987; 46: "Scranton Times," December 24, 1986; 46: interview by Angela Berryman, American Friends Service Committee, 1982; 53: Dr. Glenn Randall; 53 and 60: *Days and Nights of Love and War*, Eduardo Galeano (translator, Judith Brister), Monthly Review Press, New York, 1983; 54: interview by Ricardo Chavira; 54: interview by Jennifer Schirmer, Wellesley College; 54: "Cultural Survival Quarterly," Winter 1983; 56: *Guatemala: The Human Rights Record*, Amnesty International, London, 1987; 56: *Sanctuary: The New Underground Railroad*, Penny Gordon and Michael McConnell, Orbis Books, Maryknoll, New York, 1986; 60: *The Writer and Human Rights*, edited by the Toronto Arts Group for Human Rights, Lester & Orpen Dennys, Toronto, 1983; 72: based on research by Human Rights Watch and the International Committee of the Red Cross; 73: Center for Defense Information, Washington, D. C.; Congressional Research Service; 73: World Military Expenditures and Arms Transfers 1987; 76, 85: *Guatemala: Tyranny on Trial*, edited and translated by Susanne Jonas, Ed McCaughan, and Elizabeth Sutherland Martinez, Synthesis Publications, 1984; 79, 103, 104: *Shallow Graves*, Wendy Wilder Larsen and Tran Thi Nga, Random House, New York, 1986; 79: "The Spoils of Famine: Ethiopian Famine & Peasant Agriculture," Jason Clay et al, Cultural Survival, 1988; 79, 95, 98: Refugee Studies Program, Oxford University, England; 79: Oxfam America; 79, 98: *The Wind Blows Away Our Worlds*, Doris Lessing, Vintage Books, 1987; 82, 92: *Stateless in Gaza*, Paul Cossali and Clive Robson, Zed Books, London, 1986; 82, 103: *Imposing Aid*, B.E. Harrell-Bond, Oxford University Press, 1986; 82: *Refusenik*, Mark Ya Azbel, Paragon House, New York, 1987; 85: testimony courtesy JB Pictures, New York, 1988; 86, 92: *Spirit of Survival*, Gail Sheehy, William Morrow & Co., New York, 1986; 94: "Refugees," July 1987; 94: Peter Rose, Smith College; 94, 104, 112: *Forced to Move*, Renato Camarda (translators, Susan Hansell and Carmen Alegria), Solidarity Publications, San Francisco, 1985; 103, 104: "Refugees," February 1988; 106: *The Stranger Within Your Gates*, Andre Jacques, World Council of Churches, Geneva, 1986; 111: letter to U.S. Committee for Refugees; 120: Dr. Howard Rusk, "The New York Times," September 22, 1986; 122: "The Church of Guatemala: Lessons of History," Guatemalan Church in Exile, May 1987; 126: International Rescue Committee, 1988; 134: *Valient Women: In War and Exile*, edited by Sally Hayton-Keeva, City Lights Books, San Francisco, 1987; 144, 148: Lawyers Committee for Human Rights, New York, 1987; 148: "The Observer," London, January 24, 1988; 150: "Immigration Newsletter," September-October 1985; 150: *Mother of Exiles: Imprisoned in America*, Lawyers Committee with Americas Watch, New York, 1986; 150: *The Guarded Gate*, Norman L. Zucker and Naomi Flink Zucker, Harcourt, Brace, Jovanovich, San Diego, 1987; 154: *Fluchtpunkte: Menschen im Exil*, edited by Rudolf Karlen, Lenos Verlag, Basel, 1986; 156: interview by Susan Jonas, 1988.

FACT SOURCES

THE DESTRUCTION OF CENTRAL AMERICA GUATEMALA: 1: "World Refugee Survey," 1987; 2: United Nations; 3: "Refugee Issues," 1986; 4: Jean-Marie Simon, *Guatemala: Eternal Spring, Eternal Tyranny*, W.W. Norton & Co., 1987; 5—6: American Association for the Advancement of Science; 7: Urban Institute; 8—9: Juvenile Division of Supreme Court, Guatemala, cited by Washington Office on Latin America, 1985; 10—12: Americas Watch; 13: "World Refugee Survey," 1986; 14—15: INS.

Salvadoran refugees eagerly board trucks which will carry them
from Mesa Grande camp, Honduras, to the Honduran/Salvadoran border.

STAFF FOR *FORCED OUT*

Editor: Carole Kismaric

Associate Editor: Susan Jonas

Design: Wendy Byrne, Carole Kismaric, Charles Mikolaycak

Research: Caitlin Dixon, Joanne Gottesman, Sarah Jonas, Nan Richardson, Thomas Richardson, Michel Slubicki

Writers: Susan Jonas, Carole Kismaric

Copy Editor: Susan Weiley

Production: Design and Printing Productions, New York City

Negatives by: Premier Graphics Inc., New York City

Printed by: Arcata Graphics, Kingsport, Tennessee

Intern: Karen Weiner

Forced Out was produced for Human Rights Watch and The J. M. Kaplan Fund by Carole Kismaric. The publishing and distribution functions are being shared by a consortium of publishers:

William Morrow & Co., USA

W.W. Norton & Co., USA

Penguin Books Ltd., UK

Random House, Inc., USA

EL SALVADOR: 1: "World Refugee Survey," 1987; 2: United Nations, 1984; 3: Pan American Health Organization, 1983; 4—7: Socorro Juridico and Tutela Legal, San Salvador: 8—9: nongovernmental Human Rights Commission of El Salvador, San Salvador; 10—11: Americas Watch; 12: "Harper's Index," Henry Holt & Co., 1986; 13: U.S. Agency for International Development; 14: Americas Watch; 15: "World Refugee Survey," 1987; 16: Americas Watch; 17—18: British Refugee Council, 1986; 19—21: Arms Control and Foreign Policy Caucus, Washington, D.C., 1987; 22: Pan American Health Organization; 23: British Refugee Council; 24: UNHCR; 25—26: U.S. Immigration and Naturalization Service; 27: Lawyers Committee for Human Rights; 28: U.S. Embassy in San Salvador, cited in "The New York Times," April 13, 1987; 29—31: Arms Control and Foreign Policy Caucus; 32—33: British Refugee Council. NICARAGUA: 1: "World Refugee Survey," 1987; 2: Americas Watch; 3: United Nations; 4—7: "Washington Post," January 22, 1988; 8—9: Central American Historical Institute, quoting Nicaraguan National Institute of Statistics and Census; 10: Witness for Peace; 11—16: "American Journal of Public Health," May 1987; 17: "Miami Herald," January 31, 1988; 18—21: Americas Watch; 22: UNHCR; 23: Americas Watch; 24—27: Linda S. Peterson, "Central American Refugee Flows 1978—84," cited in the U.S. Bureau of the Census, March 1985; 28: "World Refugee Survey," 1987; 29: Americas Watch; 30—31: INS.

LIFE IN THE WORLD'S REFUGEE CAMPS

1—3: Professor Barry Stein, Department of Social Science, Michigan State University; 4: British Refugee Council; 5: "World Refugee Survey," 1987; 6—7: U.S. Committee for Refugees; 8: UNHCR; 9: "Minneapolis Star Tribune," September 16, 1987; 10: UNRWA; 11: Barry Stein; 12: UNHCR; 13—14: "Refugees," August 1987; 15: Center for Disease Control, Atlanta, Georgia; 16: UNHCR; 17—18: *Refugees—Dynamics of Displacement*, Zed Books, London, 1986; 19—21: U.S. Committee for Refugees. ETHIOPIANS: 1: World Refugee Survey, 1987; 2: "Ethiopia—Behind the Famine," Oxfam America, Facts for Action; 3—4: "Behind the Headlines—Refugees in the Horn of Africa," U.S. Committee for Refugees, January 1988; 5: "Famine, Early Warning System," U.S. Agency for International Development; 6: "Ethiopia—Behind the Famine"; 7—8: UNHCR Fact Sheet; 9: "Behind the Headlines—Refugees in the Horn of Africa"; 10: UNHCR; 11: UNHCR Fact Sheet, April 1988; 12—13: UNHCR. CAMBODIANS: 1—3: U.S. Committee for Refugees; 4: Tony Jackson, "Just Waiting to Die? Cambodian Refugees in Thailand," Oxfam, England; 5—6: U.S. Committee for Refugees; 7: Tony Jackson, "Just Waiting to Die?"; 8—9: Dr. Josephine Reynell, "Socio-Economic Evaluation of the Khmer Camps on the Thai-Kampuchean Border," Oxford, England; 10: Tony Jackson, "Just Waiting to Die?"; VIETNAMESE: 1: "The New York Times," September 12, 1988; 2—3: UNHCR; 4: U.S. Committee for Refugees; 5—7: "The New York Times," September 12, 1988; 8: "The New York Times," June 16, 1988; 9: "The World Refugee Survey", 1987; 10: UNHCR; 11: U.S. Committee for Refugees; 12—13: UNHCR; 14: "World Refugee Survey," 1987. PALESTINIANS: 1—6: UNRWA; 7—9: "Refugees," September 1987; 10—11: "Time," January 25, 1988; 12—13: UNRWA; 14: U.S. Committee for Refugees; 15—16: "Time," January 25, 1988; 17—18: UNRWA; 19: "Time," January

25, 1988; 20: West Bank Data Project, quoted in "The New York Times," December 27, 1987. AFGHANS: 1—2: Parkistan Mission to the U.N.; 3: "World Refugee Survey," 1987; 4—5: Pakistan Mission to the U.N.; 6: Afghan Media Resource Center, Peshawar, Pakistan; 7: Webster Study, Webster University, Geneva; 8—9: "The New York Times"; 10—11: Pakistan Mission; 12—13: "Frontier Review," Volume 1, No. 1; 14: "Plight of the Afghan Refugees in Pakistan, Iran, and Turkey," August 1986; 15: "Humanitarian Assistance Program for Afghan Refugees in North West Frontier Provinces," Afghan Refugee Commissionerate, Peshawar, 1987; 16: "The New York Times," November 11, 1987; 17—19: "Refugee Reports," April 15, 1988. MOZAMBICANS: 1: U.S. Committee for Refugees; 2: "World Refugee Survey," 1987; 3—4: U.S. Committee for Refugees; 5: "World Refugee Survey," 1987; 6—9: U.S. Committee for Refugees; 10: "World Refugee Survey," 1987; 11: "The New York Times," May 21, 1988; 12—13: U.S. Committee for Refugees.

XENOPHOBIA IN THE FIRST WORLD

1—3: "The Economist," April 18, 1987; 4: European Consultation on Refugees and Exiles; 5: Amnesty (France) and U.S. Committee for Refugees; 6: "Report on Irregular Movements," Gilbert Jaeger, UNHCR, 1985; 7: *Refugees: Dynamics of Displacement*, Zed Books, London, 1986; 8: "Refugees," April 1987; 9: Danish Refugee Council, 1988; 10: "Refugees," July 1987; 11: Amnesty (France) and Lawyers Committee for Human Rights; 12: U.S. Committee for Refugees. UNITED KINGDOM: 1: UNHCR; 2—3: "World Refugee Survey," 1987; 4: "The Economist," April 18, 1987; 5: European Consultation on Refugees and Exiles; 6: "World Refugee Survey," 1987; 7: "Refugees," July 1987; 8: "World Refugee Survey," 1987; 9—10: *Refugees: Dynamics of Displacement*, Zed Books, London, 1986. WEST GERMANY: 1: "World Refugee Survey," 1987; 2—4: UNHCR; 5: The New York Times," July 25, 1986; 6—7: Rudolf Klever. SWITZERLAND: 1: U.S. Committee for Refugees; 2—3: UNHCR; 4: "Refugees," January 1987; 5—6: "World Refugee Survey," 1987. SCANDINAVIA: 1: U.S. Committee for Refugees; 2—3: UNHCR; 4: "Refugees," June 1987; 5—6: UNHCR; 7—8: "Refugees," June 1987; 9: "The Economist," April 18, 1987. FRANCE: 1: UNHCR; 2: Amnesty (France); 3—6: OFPRA, Paris, 1988; 7: "Chronique d'informations internationales," Fall 1987, Paris. CANADA: 1—3: UNHCR; 4—6: "World Refugee Survey," 1987. UNITED STATES: 1: World Refugee Survey," 1987; 2: U.S. Committee for Refugees; 3—5: U.S. Immigration and Naturalization Service; 6—7: Lawyers Committee for Human Rights; 8: INS; 9: U.S. Committee for Refugees; 10—11: Lawyers Committee; 12: U.S. Committee for Refugees; 13—17: "The New York Times," July 17, 1987; 18: "The New York Times," February 15, 1987; 19: U.S. Committee for Refugees; 20—21: Lawyers Committee; 22—24: "The New York Times," November 17, 1987; 25—28: Lawyers Committee; 28—30: "Sanctuary Congregations" and "Basta!," December 1987; 31: "Public Attitudes on Refugees," U.S. Committee for Refugees; 32: "Los Angeles Times," poll September 1988.

All rights reserved under International and Pan-
American Copyright Conventions. Published in the
United States and England by Human Rights Watch
and The J. M. Kaplan Fund

Library of Congress Cataloging-in-Publication Date

ISBN: 0-679-72347-1 (Random House)
ISBN: (0-14-012086-6) (Penguin Books Ltd.)

Manufactured in the United States of America

First Edition

Forced Out is distributed in the United States by
Random House, Inc., New York; simultaneously in
Canada by Random House of Canada Limited, To-
ronto and in the United Kingdom and Europe, Ireland,
Africa, Australia, New Zealand, and India by Penguin
Books Ltd.

Every effort has been made to verify the facts and
statistics that document the refugees' experiences
in *Forced Out*. However, the movement of refugees
and their circumstances worldwide constantly
change. Data included in the publication reflect the
situation as of November 1988.

On his way home from Mexico to Guatemala, a refugee boy glimpses
for the first time in five years the mountains of his homeland.